RULERS OF THE RING

RULERS
OF THE RING

Wrestling's
Hottest
Superstars

ROBERT PICARELLO

BERKLEY BOULEVARD BOOKS, NEW YORK

RULERS OF THE RING

A Berkley Boulevard Book / published by arrangement with
the author

PRINTING HISTORY
Berkley Boulevard trade paperback edition / August 2000

The Penguin Putnam Inc. World Wide Web site address is
http://www.penguinputnam.com

ISBN: 0-425-17780-7

BERKLEY BOULEVARD
Berkley Boulevard Books are published by The Berkley Publishing Group,
a division of Penguin Putnam Inc., 375 Hudson Street, New York,
New York 10014.
BERKLEY BOULEVARD and its logo
are trademarks belonging to Penguin Putnam Inc.

PRINTED IN THE UNITED STATES OF AMERICA

10 9 8 7 6 5 4 3 2 1

I would first like to dedicate this book to the two people who made me who I am today, my mom and dad, Joan and Charles Picarello. Thank you for always being there for me and know that I love the two of you more than words can ever say.

Secondly, I would like to dedicate this book to Denise Silvestro, for without her love and inspiration both the pages in this book and my life would be empty.

Contents

Acknowledgments

WITHOUT the help and guidance of two special people, Tom Colgan and Kelly Sinanis, *Rulers of the Ring* would probably still be just a thought as opposed to a finished work. These gifted editors helped a rookie author feel like a seasoned veteran and for this I will be forever grateful.

I am also grateful for the love and support I received from my family and friends during my work on this challenging project. There are not enough pages on this earth to hold all the words of gratitude I have for all of you. Know that somewhere in the some 50,000-odd words that follow, there lies a piece of each of you.

Again, thanks goes out to: William Picarello, Charles Picarello, William Picarello, Jr., Rose Picarello, Diane Picarello, Kathleen Cassiliano, Guy Cassiliano, Gary Cassiliano, Steven Cassiliano, Gregg Cassiliano, Marianne Cassiliano, Jill Cassiliano, Kimberly Cassiliano, Kristin Cassiliano, William Brindisi, Barbara Cassiliano, Taylor Cassiliano, Marina Cassiliano, Catherina Cassiliano, (the real) Robert Picarello, Carmine (Batman) Picarello, Anthony Picarello, Nicholas Picarello, Roberta Berdel, Jodi Frunzi, Gary Scarcella, Anthony Insogna, David Stolfi, Karen Carzo, Irina Cytowicz, Joe

Pinto, Anthony Di Giovanni, Tarah O'Brien, Robert Alvarez, Dov Teta, Chuck O'Donnell, Joe Marano, Jeff Schwartzenberg, Karin Strelec, Lou Venturino, Keith Soutar, Bernard Ryan, Adam Giever, Tommy Matthews, Mark Rubenfeld, Charles Joyce, Jim Breiden-bach, Brian Doyle, Phil Mellea, Joe Delasho and Steve Ciacciarelli.

And a very special thanks goes out to my watchful eyes-in-the-sky: Guido Cassiliano, Nancy Picarello, Joseph Picarello Sr. & Jr., and Mary Daskal. Know that you are always on my mind and in my heart.

Introduction

WRESTLING has undergone a twenty-first-century makeover. No longer must grappling fanatics feel embarrassed about admitting to tuning in to the once closet-viewed sport. Wrestling is bigger and badder than ever. And wrestling fans are not ashamed to show their support. The pro wrestling federations are definitely making some noise—and money—from their *Rulers of the Ring*.

The monsters of the mat are not only busy breaking bones in the squared circle. They are also kicking ass all the way to the bank, as wrestling-related product sales are at an all-time high. The World Wrestling Federation (WWF) alone projects their sales to be somewhere in the $340 million range this year. Not too shabby for an industry that was mocked and frowned upon several years back. This boom lies mainly on the broad shoulders of these awesome athletes who put their life on the line each night for the sake of the fans and the glory, as they combine their impressive athletic abilities with loud rock music, laser-light displays, show-stopping pyrotechnics, and R-rated story lines.

These days the grappling game is no longer considered a

sport. Its image has changed over the past few years, and everyone knows that the outcomes are predetermined, but no one seems to care. The numbers don't lie. The WWF's *Raw Is War* show, which airs on cable's USA network, draws about five million viewers just on Monday nights alone. And the digits for UPN's Thursday night show, *SmackDown*, read even better for the prosperous federation. World Championship Wrestling (WCW) isn't far behind, with their combined weekly programs reaching over three million viewers.

When wrestling changed its format from sport to sports entertainment, no one could have projected the unbelievable outcome. The federations knew that the changes would allow them more room to develop their stars and plots in soap operalike fashion, but they surely didn't expect their product to outdraw the soap operas!

The makeover allowed superstars like Stone Cold Steve Austin, Goldberg, Kevin Nash, The Rock, Sting, Mankind, Chyna and many others to expand on their God-given ring abilities and come up with personalities that would drive the fans crazy. These Rulers of the Ring sure know how to energize a crowd and are the main reason why wrestling is where it is today!

Today the wrestling faithful don't care if they get a "Hell, yeah!" or the middle finger from Stone Cold, as long as the badass grappler gives them some kind of response. They love watching The Rock "lay the smack down" on his opponents or listening to Goldberg ask "Who's next?" These colorful characters each have their own following, reasons and story as to how and why they got into the business, which is hotter than ever nowadays.

Rulers of the Ring takes you on a rare backstage tour into the lives of some of today's biggest wrestling stars. You will learn about the background of each individual, how they broke into the mat game and also what lies ahead in their starry futures.

Inside you will also find a section on the *Heat Generators*, the modern-day wrestlers who like to stir the pot to keep things interesting, a *Tag Team* section on the backgrounds of some of today's dynamic duos, a *Be on the Lookout For* section, spotlighting some of the up and coming stars of the future and a *Did You Know?* section, which gives you some cool facts about the mat warriors that you might not have known!

So sit back, relax, pop open a cold one, and let's get ready to hail the Rulers of the Ring!

"Stone Cold" Steve Austin

REAL NAME: Steve Williams

HEIGHT: 6'2"

WEIGHT: 252 lbs.

BIRTHPLACE: Victoria, Texas

FINISHING MOVE: The Stone Cold Stunner

FAVORITE QUOTE: "And that's the bottom line, 'cause Stone Cold said so!"

THE sound of breaking glass echoing in the wrestling world can only mean one of two things—either "Stone Cold" Steve Austin is making his way into the ring, or the WWF superstar just opened up another can of "whoop ass" on another unfortunate foe.

This six-foot two, 252-pound wrestling phenom has taken the wrestling world by storm, and there's no slowing him down. No matter the size, shape, weight, height or grappling background of the competition, Stone Cold has disposed of his ring opponents like none before him.

Just the mere mention of the Victoria, Texas native's name brings sold-out arenas into a frenzy. When the beer-guzzling wrestler struts into the ring, everyone is guaranteed to be entertained. But if they're not and he says or does something to offend them, that's just too bad! He didn't get the tag as wrestling's "meanest S.O.B." for nothing.

"If you watch the show, I'm gonna entertain you one way or another," the rebellious wrestler has said. "If you don't like me, if you hate my guts, that's fine. It doesn't bother me at all. What you see is what you get with me."

His stern look—bald head, goatee, black trunks and boots and "rebel with a cause attitude"—are all a part of what makes up his WWF personality. Tie in all those characteristics with his awesome wrestling ability and you've got yourself the mold of one badass champion. Stone Cold's character appeals not only to the women (we all know how the ladies love the rebel) and children, but a lot of his followers are males who range from the ages of eleven to forty-five. One of the reasons he is so popular with this group is that Austin is a former blue-collar worker who is not afraid to throw down with anyone, especially his boss. Hell, this wrestler wouldn't think twice about throwing his boss down the stairs if he deserved it. And that's not only the truth, "It's the bottom line!"

Speaking of the bottom line, do you think the officials at World Championship Wrestling regret the day they let this cash cow slip through their fingers? Several years back, while Austin was working for WCW, he was fired from the federation while he was rehabbing an injury that he had sustained in the ring. The reason they gave him for his dismissal—over the phone, nonetheless—was that they didn't believe there was a future for a wrestler who wore only black trunks and black boots. Oh yeah, and he was told by those geniuses that he didn't have enough persona to be a major superstar!

According to Austin, the officials over at WCW treated him like a "complete jackass," and he was determined to prove them wrong.

"The success I've had is awesome," he explained, "and I can't say enough about it. I've paid the price to get here and being on top is a good thing, but I want to stay there. I don't want a short run."

It took many years for Steve Austin, a.k.a. Steve Williams, to get to where he is today. In 1989, the future WWFer was living in Texas and working on the docks loading and unloading trucks. He had just graduated from North Texas State University (now the University of North Texas) where he not only got an education, but also played for their Division 1–AA football team on an athletic scholarship. But those credentials alone weren't going to pay his bills at the end of the month when he graduated from college. Williams wasn't drafted by a pro football team, and he needed to earn cash like every other person, so he turned to the docks for a while.

The former college football gridiron great had always been a fan of wrestling. In his leisure time he loved going to the Sportatorium in Dallas to watch the Von Erichs wrestle. While he was growing up, he always watched Paul Boesch's Houston Wrestling program on television. It must have been fate when, one day, while Williams was reading the paper after work, he stumbled upon an ad in the classified section for a wrestling school run by Chris Adams.

"I just figured 'Hell, if those guys could do it, I could do it, too,' " the future wrestler said.

Without hesitation he clipped the ad and brought it home and phoned the school and enrolled. Little did he know that five months later he would be stepping between the ropes against some of his classmates, taking part in his first professional wrestling match.

He first broke in with World Class Championship Wrestling, which in reality was far from world class, but he liked it way better than working the docks. He put in his time with the minor league organization, but eventually he had to get out. Not only was the money bad, but he also developed a major rivalry with one of the other grapplers—none other than his mentor, Chris Adams. The two engaged in a bitter "feud" which actually ended up with the student overtaking the teacher.

"When you first get out into the ring, you're nervous as hell. When I first started, you were wrestling in front of a couple of hundred people or maybe a thousand and I was making $20 a night. It's a hell of a feeling," he said.

The battles actually didn't only involve the two wrestlers. Sometimes Adams's wife Tori and his ex-girlfriend Jeanie Clark got involved. Clark aligned herself with Williams and the two would become inseparable both in and out of the ring after their meeting. Tori and Jeanie would do more than stand by their men when they appeared at ringside. The two voluptuous women would also engage in some fierce battles between the ropes that were sometimes better than the men's battles.

While Jeanie was proving that she could handle herself in the ring, Williams was not only handling himself, he was also developing into a hell of a wrestler. But he knew he was still far away from the big time and that he still had to pay his dues.

In 1991, World Championship Wrestling came calling. Williams made his WCW debut as "Stunning" Steve Austin. He would come into the ring sporting the gorgeous valet Lady Blossom (Jeanie Clark, who would also become his real-life wife) on his muscular arm while his long, blond hair flowed in the arena air. The sight was far from "stunning." Williams may as well have been called "Boring" Steve Austin, because that's what this character was.

While he may have been boring the piss out of the crowd, he still managed to rack up the wins and belts along the way. In the five years he spent with WCW, "the stunning one" managed to garner three different belts at different times. In June 1991, he would win his first championship title. With Blossom still by his side, he captured the organization's TV Title from Bobby Eaton and held that belt until April 27 of the following year.

After the loss, Austin dumped Blossom and hooked up with the Dangerous Alliance, which was managed by Paul E. Dangerously. Under Dangerously he regained the belt a couple of weeks later on May 23, 1992, when he defeated Barry Windham. His reign lasted all the way until September 2, when Windham got his revenge and beat Austin for the right to be called TV Champ.

The second title Austin held in the federation was that of Tag Team Champion. He and his partner in crime, "Flyin' " Brian Pillman, had the distinct honor of not only wearing these belts and defeating any and all tag teams who got in their way; they were also considered one of the best tag teams in the world. The two, known as the "Hollywood Blondes," worked really well together not only in the ring, but also outside. They worked the mics like no other tandem as they were vocal, tough and exciting. On March 23, 1993, they defeated Ricky Steamboat and Shane Douglas to earn the right to be called WCW Tag Team Champs. This twosome had to be by far the highlight of Austin's career up to this point, but there were other teams and other wrestlers who were starting to resent the attention the team was getting.

"Me and Brian were the hottest team to come down the pike in quite some time," Austin said. "Everybody wanted to see the Blondes and because of that, some of the other wrestlers got jealous and got together with their little buddies in the office to hold us back. . . . Because certain people with grease were acting like a bunch of twelve-year-old girls, we got held back, meaning they were cutting their nose to spite their damn face. These veterans who thought they knew it all, couldn't see the big picture: the more tickets the Blondes sold, the better it was for everyone."

But the winds of change began to blow for the awesome duo. The following year Austin captured his third and final WCW title, as he won a singles belt with a new sidekick/manager, Colonel Robert Parker. His winning this championship signaled the beginning of the end for the Hollywood Blondes tag team. Many blamed Parker's association with Austin for the ugly breakup of The Blondes, but Austin didn't care at the time, as Parker delivered what he promised—a shot at the WCW's U.S. title. He won the WCW United States Championship on December 27 when he disposed of Dustin Rhodes, but many in the industry were still grumbling over Parker's influence on Austin's career and his part in the breakup of the tag team.

One of the first personalities to speak out at the time was

then-announcer Jesse "The Body" Ventura. "It's no secret I considered The Blondes to be the best team in the world. I didn't think there was a single team on the horizon that posed any threat to them. It brought a real tear to my eye to see them wind up going at each other. And you know us [Navy] SEALs don't tear up easily.

"On the other hand," the now-Minnesota governor continued, "it's also no secret that people are in professional wrestling to make lots of money. If 'Stunning Steve' can make more of the big green by listening to the Colonel, I can't knock him for that."

It was also no secret that the "stunning" one was a much better singles wrestler than he was as part of a tag, but Austin himself was OK with the breakup at the time. As a matter of fact, he was relieved. "I think it's quite clear that Brian Pillman was always the weak link in the team. Watch tapes of our matches and you'll see that I did 90 percent of the work for 50 percent of the glory."

"Stunning" Steve also added: "Let me make it crystal clear, I could care less about losing a tag partner. I never wanted one and never in my life did I ever need or ask somebody to watch my back. How do I feel about getting rid of Flyin' Brian? How do you feel after an abscessed tooth is yanked out of your mouth or an ingrown toenail is trimmed? Nothing but relief." He was happy to be starting this new kind of partnership with the Colonel.

From the get-go, Parker was always in Austin's corner. He truly believed that this grappler had what it took to be a big-time wrestling personality. In a 1993 interview, he told one reporter from *Wrestling World:* "My good man, you'll be writing articles about the glorious triumphs of 'Stunning' Steve for years to come. We've only just begun our conquest of the wrestling sport. I'm getting faxes and phone calls from promoters all over the world who are interested in Steve Austin. Movie producers, too."

In only his second pro season, Austin found himself amongst elite company when he strapped that U.S. Championship title belt around his waist. As a matter of fact, "Stunning" Steve held onto the belt longer than anyone who came before him. His first U.S. title lasted for a good eight months before he lost the belt to Ricky Steamboat on August 24, 1994. Later in the year, Austin also got this title back, as he was awarded the belt on September 18, 1994, when an injured Ricky Steamboat was unable to compete in a scheduled match. Thus, Austin embarked on his second tour of duty as WCW U.S. Champ. But it wasn't long after this that the federation gave him his walking papers, or at least *called* him to let him know about them.

His being fired by the WCW was by no means a highlight at the time, but when you look at where he's at today as compared to where he was then, it's safe to say that Austin was glad to get that phone call from WCW executive Eric Bischoff.

"I kept hearing how they had big plans for me down the road a piece and I was all set to kick some ass then, not two years later. Besides, you can't trust anybody in this business. . . . So, here I was, supposed to be their faired-haired boy," Austin explained, "and the next thing I know, Eric Bischoff's calling me up to tell me I'm fired. Can you believe it? He wasn't even man enough to do it face-to-face."

But Austin knew there was no use crying over spilled milk (or beer, in his case) and was man enough to move on. He hooked up with the Pennsylvania-based Extreme Championship Wrestling (ECW) for a brief time, a brand of wrestling that lived up to its very title.

Upon his leaving the WCW, Parker had nothing but good things to say about his run with Steve Austin. "Of all the men on God's green Earth I've managed—and there have been many greats—Steve Austin was the most attentive and easiest to handle. Steve is very inquisitive; always asking questions about different techniques; always trying to improve himself.

"You tell Steve Austin to do something, he does it," Parker explained. "No back talk. I've seen a lot of guys make the big leagues and suddenly think they know all there is to know about the business. Steve's not like that. And, believe me, I know from cocky."

His time spent at ECW allowed him to refocus on his wrestling career and try new things in the ring. He worked on his persona and actually wound up doing a pretty darn good impression of Hulk Hogan, where he would preach in Hulklike fashion to "say your prayers and take your vitamins."

But in late 1995, the WWF came calling! Austin inked a deal with Vince McMahon's federation and things began to change for the "badder." Although it took some time for Austin to turn "Stone Cold," he was very happy to be on board with the WWF. He knew he would be taken care of in the WWF, though he wasn't about to let his guard down.

"I'll tell ya what," he said after inking his deal, "McMahon and the rest [of the front office] better not try to put me in many tags or try to kiss up to me like we're friends or something. I'll go right up to that office and open up a whole six-pack of Whoop Ass [on them]."

Even though he was ready to pop open a couple, he also knew he was in a better situation now than he was before. The WWF was definitely not the WCW. "The similarities are that they're supposed to both be pro wrestling [organizations]. That's pretty much where it ends because we blow 'em away in every aspect of the business," Austin said. "Our attendance and product is ten times better than theirs. As far as being the place to be, the WWF gives you that opportunity."

When he first arrived, he was given the moniker the "Ring Master." Not only did the gimmick not work, but Austin was also assigned a sidekick in Ted DiBiase. This did not go over well with the former WCWer, as he prefers to be a loner, but he bit the bullet and went along with it . . . for a little while, anyway.

One of the reasons Austin was so unhappy was because he felt that the character didn't even come close to who he really was. He felt more like a circus act than a professional wrestler. "It sucked," he explained. "It [the Ring Master character] had no personality or anything and I wasn't allowed to be myself."

"When I first came up here to the WWF, some genius up in the ivory tower decided I needed a damn gimmick name and manager. So suddenly I was being called the 'Ring Master'—like I was from some circus—and they dusted off the Million Dollar Belt for me to wear and expected me to be happy using someone else's finishing maneuver."

On May 16, 1996, during a Pay-Per-View stipulation match, Austin lost a Caribbean Strap Match to Savio Vega. The stipulation tied to the match was that if the "Ring Master" lost, DiBiase would have to leave the federation.

"Well, I was none too pleased about the whole situation," Austin said, "but I was new in the WWF and kept being told,

'Don't worry, you'll be taken care of.' I was being taken, all right," he said sarcastically. "Although I hate losing, the best thing that ever happened to me at that point was dropping the match where DiBiase had to leave the WWF."

Did somebody say fix? Did the Ring Master really throw the match?

"I never needed nobody to do the talkin' for me, and I certainly didn't need some suit telling me who I should or shouldn't be challenging. That went for Ted and it goes for everybody on down," Austin said.

People in and around wrestling were about to find out that this guy was an ass kicker, not an ass kisser!

With DiBiase now out of his life, Austin felt more at ease. The only thing he was still unhappy with was his ring name. He didn't like the "Ring Master" tag at all. "Hell, I always believed if you're going to do something, you have to believe in yourself 100 percent," Austin explained. "If you don't believe in yourself or believe you can accomplish something, why even do it at all?"

But the wrestling gods must have been shining down on him, because one evening when he was talking with his then-wife Jeanie over a cup of tea (they have recently divorced), she told him to drink his beverage before it got "stone cold." Well, instead of the tea becoming "stone cold," Austin did! He adopted the moniker, and before you could say "Hell, yeah!" a hero was born.

Austin introduced "Stone Cold" to the wrestling world on the night of June 23, 1996. It was at a King of the Ring tournament where Austin would square off against Jake "The Snake" Roberts in the finals. But before he got to the finals, he cut his lip in the semifinal round in a bout against "Wildman" Marc Mero. He left the arena to get stitches to close up the wound and while he was gone Roberts ran off his mouth in a TV interview.

"Stone Cold" remembered the incident like this: "I went to the hospital to close my mouth back up and when I got back someone had informed me that Jake Roberts had done a religious interview prior to our matchup. At the time, Jake Roberts was going around the country giving religious testimonies, [and the WWF officials told him] if you win, you might use that in your King of the Ring acceptance speech.

"So, after I beat Jake 'The Snake' Roberts," Austin said, "he was walking up the aisle [and] basically what I said to a T was, 'You sit there and you thump your Bible and say your prayers and it didn't get you anywhere. You talk about your psalms. You talk about John 3:16. Well, Austin 3:16 said 'I just whipped your ass!' It was completely ad-libbed. Everything I do is basically ad-libbed. If I hadn't wrestled Jake 'The Snake' Roberts that night and someone hadn't have said he did a religious interview on me, I would have never came up with Austin 3:16 out of the blue. It wasn't anything designed to be sacreligious; just something that I said."

Austin, minus the blond locks, had now officially arrived in the WWF and he wasn't about to stop there. He wanted to get to the top so bad that he didn't care about who he had to go through to get there. He was a loner with a take-no-prisoners attitude. His attitude wasn't only toward his opponents, either. While he was gracious that he had the fans on his side, he also wanted them to know that he meant business. He couldn't allow them to turn him soft. He needed to stay focused on the tasks and opponents at hand. After all, they weren't going to help him win the belt and they also weren't going to pay his rent.

"I see these people wearing Austin 3:16 shirts," Stone Cold said. "They may try to convince you it somehow makes me feel good, but the fact of the matter is they do it to make themselves feel better. I certainly ain't benefiting much financially from it, neither. I make my money kicking ass in the ring, not selling posters."

But the diesel wrestler would do a lot of both. Stone Cold would not only rise to the top of the wrestling ranks in no time, he would also sell merchandise like none before him. Stores couldn't get enough of Austin merchandise, as the stuff was flying off the shelves faster than Austin was mauling his opponents.

He would run into and over top-notch grapplers such as "Wildman" Marc Mero, Yokozuna and Hunter Hearst Helmsley in the next couple of months. But the one matchup everybody was looking forward to was Austin versus Bret "The Hitman" Hart. The two would square off at the 1996 Survivor Series, but The Hitman would get the better of Stone Cold on this occasion. While Hart relished in his victory, Austin stewed, because the only reason Hart was able to beat Austin on this night was that Stone Cold made one big mistake in the match. At one point in the contest, Austin had Hart where he wanted him and tried to get the pin by locking The Hitman in DiBiase's "Million Dollar Dream" sleeper hold, but being the savvy veteran that he was, Hart was able to reverse the hold and gain the pin. Austin vowed never to make the same mistake again, and from then on he would only do his own exclusive maneuvers.

This was the first lockup between the two federation stars,

but it wouldn't be the last. The two locked horns over the next few months and set the stage for the big showdown at the WWF's biggest event—WrestleMania.

The WrestleMania XIII match was a memorable one because it not only featured "Stone Cold" against "The Hitman," but the contest was also labeled a submission match, where the winner has to make his opponent say, "I quit!" In order to guarantee a winner, Ken Shamrock, the submission specialist, was hired as the special guest referee. In the weeks leading up to the event Austin vowed that he would never say those words at WrestleMania.

His statement would hold true: he never did utter "I quit" during the match against Hart. Though The Hitman came out victorious on that night, it wasn't from Austin's giving in. The only reason Hart got the win was because Austin passed out from losing so much blood and Shamrock decided to stop the contest.

With revenge on his mind, Stone Cold squared off against Hart a month later and this time left the ring with a victory, even if it was by disqualification. Not feeling happy about winning by DQ, Austin challenged Hart the next night on *RAW* to a No Holds Barred Street Fight. He would finally put a lickin' on The Hitman on this night and he couldn't seem to get enough of the pounding he was giving Hart. The Hitman was taken away from the arena by ambulance, but that didn't stop Austin. He hid in the truck and proceeded to pound his helpless opponent again. This beating would cause Hart to miss the next three months of work.

Stone Cold would finally get a shot at championship gold in May 1997. He took on the mysterious Undertaker at an In Your House Event, but he again would come up empty as a blast from his WCW past finally got revenge on him. Just when it looked as though

Austin had The Undertaker beaten, his former tag partner, Brian Pillman, rang the bell early, causing the ref to become distracted. The Undertaker then applied a Tombstone piledriver to Austin and successfully defended his belt.

Stone Cold was furious. He declared war on the Hart Foundation and was not only determined to win the championship belt, but he wanted to take on the faction which not only included Pillman, but also Bret Hart, his brother Owen, the British Bulldog and Jim "The Anvil" Neidhart. Austin was going to stop at nothing for revenge. He was not going to let anyone interfere with his rise to glory. Not Pillman, not the fans . . . not anyone!

He said, "I see all these fans walking around the arenas wavin' their little signs thinking that makes us one big happy family. Well, I've got Austin verse 4:16 for them: This is wrestling, not a damn episode of *Friends*. You pat my back, I'll kick your ass too . . . just like I'm gonna do to that whining Bret Hart, the Hart Foundation, The Undertaker, pretty boy [Shawn] Michaels and anybody else who wants to get in Steve Austin's face. And that's the bottom line because Stone Cold says so!"

His first chance at revenge came on May 27, 1997, when he would team up with one of his bitter rivals, "The Heartbreak Kid" Shawn Michaels. In a tag-team match against the then-reigning champions, Owen Hart and The British Bulldog, the bitter grappler put his rivalry with Michaels aside for a night and teamed up with him just for a chance to beat Owen and Bulldog. Austin would not only get his first taste of revenge on the Hart Foundation members, but he would also get his first taste of WWF gold when he and Michaels defeated Hart and The Bulldog for the right to be called tag-team champions.

Being the loner that he is, Austin just couldn't get along with his tag partner Michaels. As a matter of fact, the two faced each other in a King of the Ring event that year in June. Though the match ended in a double disqualification, it wouldn't be the last time the two foes would meet between the ropes.

Due to an injury to The Heartbreak Kid, the duo was stripped of their belts, and a tournament would take place to determine who would have the right to wear the championship belts. The winners would also have to face Austin and a partner of his choice on a July 14, 1997, edition of *RAW*.

Being the busy (and marked) man that he was, Austin had other things—mainly revenge—on his mind before he could even think about the tag match. He teamed with the Legion of Doom, Ken Shamrock and Goldust to take on the Hart Foundation in an In Your House event. The ten-man showdown wound up being a half-hour war, which finally ended with Owen Hart, the then-reigning Intercontinental Champion, pinning Austin. Stone Cold was again enraged and promised to get even with Hart.

Naturally, Owen and The British Bulldog won the tag tournament for the right to face Austin and his unannounced partner in July. When the fourteenth rolled around, however, Stone Cold came alone. But a few moments after Austin's entrance, to everyone's surprise, up popped Dude Love, who made his way into the ring. The duo teamed up and beat the Hart Foundation members to a pulp and claimed the championship.

But Austin wasn't done. He still had more gold and revenge on his mind. Next stop was Intercontinental Championship Road. Stone Cold would venture up this path not only because he wanted to add another belt to his list, but also because he wanted to knock Owen Hart off the throne.

Stone Cold challenged the younger Hart to a championship match at SummerSlam and vowed that if he couldn't beat him on that night, he would "kiss his ass" right in the center of the ring.

Again in typical Stone Cold fashion, the Texas Rattlesnake went about his business, and there was no ass kissing on this night, just ass kicking. But this victory over Owen Hart for the championship would be a bittersweet one for Austin. The sweet part of that night at the 1997 SummerSlam was that Austin won his first single's title. The bitter part of the night came when Owen attempted a piledriver on Austin, and Stone Cold landed awkwardly. The injury not only hurt that night; it would be career-threatening to the bald wrestler. Despite being in tremendous pain, the courageous grappler was still somehow able to roll over and get the pin on Hart.

"When I hit," Austin recalled, "the first thing that popped into my mind was Christopher Reeve. I never thought I would move again. It scared the hell out of me, but the weird thing was I never lost consciousness and my mind was crystal clear. For a minute, I couldn't move my arms or legs and then finally, slowly, I could see out of the side of my eyes that my fingers started to move. I was thinking to myself, 'Well, that's good.' And I got out of the match."

Injury again would play a role in Austin being stripped of one of his titles as he was declared ineligible to compete because of his own health status. Although he would not wrestle for a while, Austin still managed to get involved in the outcome of some matches—particularly those that involved Owen Hart.

During a tag-title match, Austin interfered and helped the

Headbangers become champs as he made his way to the ring during the contest and applied a Stone Cold stunner to Hart to help make his duo lose. On another occasion, Stone Cold interfered in a match between Owen Hart and Faarooq, but this time he would help Hart get the win. Why—because Stone Cold knew so! Austin knew he was going to be back in action a few weeks later and he wanted to be able to uncrown Hart himself and become the new Intercontinental Champion (IC).

At the 1997 Survivor Series, Austin would do just that and he would again become IC champ. He would defend his title in December against another wrestler with whom he would become bitter enemies—"The Rock." One night after this title defense, he was again asked to take on The Rock on *RAW*, but he refused and, instead handed over the strap to the young grappler, claiming he had bigger fish to fry. He would give up the title to this young wrestler so he could focus his energies elsewhere.

He was now going full-force for the heavyweight championship.

Austin would go on to win the 1998 Royal Rumble, which immediately qualified him to become eligible for a title match against Shawn Michaels at WrestleMania XIV. Even though the odds were stacked against him, as Vince McMahon didn't want Austin as his federation champ, Stone Cold would come away with the victory over Michaels in Boston at WrestleMania and thus start a new chapter in WWF championship history.

Even though Austin was ecstatic to be the champion, McMahon was not. He was determined to do everything in his power to knock Stone Cold off his podium. Dude Love was the first grappler to take a shot at Austin, but the hippie wrestler couldn't take the title from the meanest wrestler in the federation. The Big Red

Machine, Kane, was the next title-hungry wrestler to go after Stone Cold, and he actually beat Austin in a First Blood Match at the 1998 King of the Ring event. But Kane wouldn't hold the title for long, as Austin quickly got his belt back the next night on *RAW*.

The more roadblocks McMahon would put in front of Austin, the more the two-time champ would tear them down. Over the next nine months, the Austin/McMahon feud was in full force. The two even tangled inside the ring a couple of times, which not only made for memorable matches, but also great TV. Austin was more and more becoming a cult hero, as he truly was winning the battle of the employee vs. the employer!

Austin would battle for his third championship in March 1999 at WrestleMania against another of McMahon's hand-picked boys—The Rock. Austin promised to check Rocky Maivia into Room 316 of the Smackdown Hotel "and burn the son of a bitch to the ground" when he was through with him. Stone Cold would win his third title belt that night in Philadelphia, which again pissed off his boss.

After The Rock's unsuccessful attempts of stripping Austin of the belt, next came The Undertaker. The mean warrior would unseat Austin and become WWF champion for the third time in his dark career. But Austin wasn't going to take losing the championship lying down. He battled The Undertaker at a Fully Loaded event in Charlotte, North Carolina, and won his fourth heavyweight title.

He lost the belt two months later at SummerSlam in Minneapolis in a Triple Threat Match, which included him, Mankind and Triple H. Mankind would walk away with the belt, but Austin vowed to be back.

Austin again suffered another career-threatening injury and

was forced to undergo surgery in mid-January 2000 in San Antonio, Texas. Although his surgery was reported to be a complete success, one has to wonder how much more punishment his body can endure. Stone Cold agrees that any time you step through those ropes, it could be your last. "I have to be careful what I do these days and watch what kind of predicament I put myself into. You never know. Everybody has their own opinion about pro wrestling, but I'll tell you this, anytime you go into the ring, it might be your last. And that's the truth."

The truth is, there has never been any other wrestler like Steve Austin, and for those of you who are counting him out, don't— because Stone Cold said so!

Chyna

REAL NAME: **Joanie Laurer**

HEIGHT: **5'9"**

WEIGHT: **185 lbs.**

BIRTHPLACE: **Rochester, New York**

FINISHING MOVE: **The Pedigree**

FAVORITE ATHLETE: **Mike Tyson**

THE quote "Behind every great man is an even greater woman," is a saying that needs to be altered to "Behind every great federation is an even greater woman," when referring to the World Wrestling Federation's beautiful ring queen Chyna.

Born Joanie Laurer in Rochester, New York, on December 27, 1970, the chiseled Chyna isn't only about brawn, beauty and bullying. As a matter of fact, she's more about surviving. The WWF's number one lady didn't have an easy childhood.

Any typical child might have gone into a shell under the unfortunate circumstances of living in a broken home and being estranged from family members, but Laurer is no ordinary girl. When looking back, the hardest pill for her to swallow was that both of her parents were very well educated and had business savvy, yet she felt they didn't know how to raise a family.

Her mother was an executive for a large corporation and her father was a successful businessman, but that didn't help their home life. In an interview with *RAW* magazine, Laurer described her mom as being "a psycho co-dependent who had revolving door marriages," and she also explained that her dad had problems with alcohol. But she was tough way beyond her years, and she decided from a young age that she was going to come out of this situation not only successful, but normal.

When Joanie was fifteen, her mom was convinced that her daughter was on drugs because of her erratic behavior, so she forced her to check into a rehab center. The counselors realized that this wasn't the case and discharged her pretty quickly. Upon being released, the young, confused girl sought help from her dad, who at this time was sober and remarried.

Besides having the mental toughness to get through this hard time in her life, Laurer also had many very important characteristics going for her: she was a very good student, had a very cheerful personality, and was very athletic.

She moved in with her dad and took up weightlifting. She also spent time in Europe for two years with the intent of exploring new worlds, and more importantly, of finding herself. While trekking through Europe with her dad and his new wife, she learned to speak three languages—French, German and Spanish. One night many years later, she got the chance to show off her Spanish-speaking skills on an episode of *RAW*.

When she returned to the States, she enrolled in the University of Tampa, where she majored in foreign languages. She did well at Tampa, but she ached to get back to Europe. In her senior year, the well-traveled student spent the final six months of her college career studying abroad in Spain to finish off her major. Laurer also explained that she ran away from the States to get away from her home life again. She claimed that her dad took out school loans which left her $40,000 in debt.

After graduating from the University of Tampa, the bright young lady had no desire to go home, so she joined the Peace Corps in 1992. For a while she even considered a career as a diplomat or as a member of the U.S. Secret Service. But she would soon leave the Corps and the classroom behind and decide to pursue a career in bodybuilding.

Besides making a name for herself at the time in her own gym, she was also being noticed in the fitness world by talent scouts. She worked her body into such tremendous shape that she earned the reputation as one of the up-and-coming competitors in the business.

In 1995, she met a fitness promoter by the name of Kenny Kassell, who would become instrumental not only in her bodybuilding career, but in her new wrestling career. She mentioned to Kassell that she was interested in pursuing a career in professional wrestling and he immediately offered to help, even though he felt she had a better chance at making a more lucrative career in fitness competitions.

It would be a tough road for the future WWFer. Women's wrestling was basically looked down upon by the big promoters and many of the indie leagues. But Laurer knew what she was getting into and besides, she now had something she had lacked growing up—someone in her corner who believed in her. And that someone was Kassell.

Even though he knew modern-day professional wrestling organizations weren't really scouting around for women grapplers—as they were more interested in the women who could look good outside the ring instead of inside—he still offered his services. He made some calls and put Laurer in touch with Randy Powell, the founder of the Professional Girl Wrestling Association (PGWA), who also worked at an entertainment organization known as Special Events. This contact would be key for this future woman wrestler because this North Carolina–based organization not only promoted all-female wrestling events, they also supported the sport by creating both professional and amateur women's wrestling publications and videos.

Seeing the potential and physique Laurer had, Powell agreed to help train her. But he had a major task on his hands with the former fitness competitor, because she knew little about the sport of wrestling. She may have wanted to become a wrestler, but she had no idea how to wrestle!

"It was no easy task, unfortunately," Powell admitted to *WOW* magazine. "She knew nothing about [the sport of] wrestling. I wanted to have her train in North Carolina and was seeking some financial backing for her room, board and trainers. [But] I found it nearly impossible to find assistance because no one had heard of her and they weren't impressed with her fitness background. 'Oh, a bodybuilder,' they would say and they would just lose all interest."

Powell even had intentions of sending Laurer to the mid-

Atlantic to train with a pro wrestler who had her own wrestling school, but again he ran into the problem of not being able to round up the funds to help sponsor her. "I had wanted her to train with pro wrestler Susan Green at her school and work with other independent promoters who also offer training, but I could not find anyone in the mid-Atlantic area willing to sponsor her," he said.

Little did Powell know that Laurer had been through worse in her life. She was not about to give up that easily. He was dealing with a woman who, at one time in her life, decided to take the firefighter's test in her adopted hometown of Boston, Massachusetts, just because it would pose a challenge. Even though this test was taken predominantly by men, she didn't care. "The firefighters physical test was the most challenging event I have ever been exposed to," Joanie explained. So finding a sponsor or someone to train her was going to be a piece of cake in comparison to taking that exam.

When she learned of "Killer" Kowalski's wrestling school in Massachusetts, she was all set to become a student again, only this time she'd be using her brawn instead of her brains. The Hall of Fame wrestler had retired from the ring and was now making his living teaching other wrestlers how to make it between the ropes. He was a ringmaster who knew the sport in and out. Wanna-be pros, both men and women, came from all over to be trained by him. Several women who were taught by the Hall of Famer, including Violet Flame, Amanda Storm, Misty Blue Simmes and Brittany Brown all went on to have good careers between the ropes.

Excited about the idea of training with this wrestling great, Laurer decided to enroll in the beginning of 1996. During her training days at the Kowalski School, she learned to wrestle with several other grapplers whom she would meet again down the road in her pro career. But the one who stood out the most, and who would help her most, was Hunter Hearst Helmsley. But more on him later.

The wanna-be female wrestler was quickly picking up the sport, and everyone around her knew she was destined to be someone special in the business. In addition to the numerous power moves she learned from Kowalski, Laurer would perfect a back handspring elbow smash and a suffocating bear hug.

Kowalski loved having Laurer as his student. "She was always hardworking and very pleasant to be around. Joanie has a great sense of humor, but when she gets down to work, her attitude is a kick-ass, no joking style."

Now that she had the training, it was time to test out her skills in the ring.

The next stop on her journey to the pros would be Las Vegas, Nevada. In 1996, she attended the Ladies International Wrestling Association's (LIWA) convention as a guest of Powell. This would be the perfect place to introduce her to members of the media, promoters and anybody else who could help her career get started. Powell's plan started to work. Many people, especially the promoters, were beginning to take notice of Laurer when they heard that she was not only being endorsed by the PGWA, but that she had also been trained by Killer Kowalski.

Laurer was having the time of her life, as she was not only meeting people in her new industry and impressing them, but she also was signing autographs, something she got a great big kick out of doing. She was happy to be getting her feet wet, and ecstatic about being accepted and noticed.

Powell recalled, "As I introduced Joanie to those in attendance, people knew she was a real pro wrestler and not just a wanna-be who had crashed the convention." Powell continued, "I guess the guests at this convention instinctively knew, like I knew, that this girl was destined for success. And that the fans who attended that event have something that few people of today have, and that's the ability to say 'I knew her when.' "

Another Special Events employee, Tom Randolph, also remembers Laurer as being an attention-getter. "She takes to public relations like ducks take to water. Joanie is one of those athletes who has the ability to make friends and make fans feel at ease around her. She is a definite role model for wrestling, fitness, firefighting or whatever she does."

But even though she had the meet-and-greets down pat, she still wasn't battle-tested in the ring, and Powell knew that. He knew that in order for her to really get noticed in the industry, he had to get her on a mat and squaring off against an opponent before the convention was over.

Powell worked every angle and every source he knew to get Laurer a shot. Just when it seemed like he would come up empty, he ran into the president of the LIWA, Lillian Ellison. He had been trying all along to convince Ellison to put Laurer on one of her cards, but she wasn't biting.

"I had offered Lillian Ellison the chance to have Joanie on the live card they held at the convention, but she declined," Powell said. "Of course, who could blame her for saying no? No one except me knew who Joanie was, what she could do, or if she could handle a pro match."

But after some more begging and pleading, Powell was able to secure a spot for Laurer on the live card. She would be wrestling another newcomer, Angie Jenet. "How ashamed I would have felt to have promoted someone that hard, encouraging her to come to Las Vegas and expose herself to potential criticism, and then failed to provide her with the showcase she deserved. I persuaded Lillian to let Joanie have a preliminary match against another newcomer, and if that went well, she might be able to participate in a mixed tag-team match later in the card."

Not surprisingly, Laurer kicked some serious butt and was the star of the card.

"Needless to say, Joanie was the star of the show," said Powell. "Every fan loved the match she had. Angie Jenet was Joanie's opponent and I am sure Jenet will always be proud of this match. Angie was also a talented rookie, but she couldn't match Joanie's strength and ended up breaking her nose. She put up a good fight, but Joanie won the match."

Having put on a good show and winning, Laurer earned the right to wrestle again that night. This time she would grapple in a mixed tag match with a male partner against the very powerful Psycho Cybil. Psycho or not, Laurer kicked her foe's butt and again impressed those in attendance. Her career had now arrived and she was ready to keep on moving forward.

Laurer, who wrestled under the ring moniker of Joanie Lee, quickly made a name and enemies for herself around the women's circuit. The well-trained and conditioned wrestler was usually too powerful for her opponents, and would dispose of them rather quickly. Special Events and the PGWA were thriving with Laurer participating in their organizations. She was frequently gracing the pages of their magazine *LadySports* and her videotaped matches were one of their bestsellers.

She was quite a different personality when she first hit the mat scene. Today's WWF fans would be shocked to know that she began her wrestling career with an All-American girl look (that would explain her red, white and blue outfit). Lee not only had a squeaky-clean look outside the ring in her early days, she was also a wrestle-by-the-rules type of gal between the ropes. She only knew one way to wrestle—fair and square.

That was until she made her way down to sunny Florida to wrestle for the Universal Wrestling Federation (UWF) in the fall of 1996. While in the sunshine state, she would not only begin to change her wrestling style and ring appearance (her hair went from red to black); she would also run into some steep competition. The UWF had two stars in Liz Chase and Riptide, who were notorious not only for breaking their competition's heads, but also for breaking the rules. Lee built up a pretty heated rivalry with Riptide during her time in the sun.

The ultimate battle between the two came at an all-girl wrestling card at the Iron Horse Saloon in Daytona Beach. The contest between the bitter rivals was caught on tape because Special Events was present shooting a video called *Wild Women at the Iron Horse*. The match had all the hype of a championship fight and the viewers would not be disappointed. Riptide was unlike Lee's competition up until then; she had a legitimate shot at beating her new foe. Riptide had a shootfighting background and, like her PGWA counterpart, was also into bodybuilding.

The Floridian would put up a great fight—and would break every rule under the sun—with Lee, who was no angel herself that night in the ring. In the end, the Killer Kowalski–trained grappler would earn the victory.

As for her change in style, Lee had this to say: "Everyone was

breaking the rules . . . and I just saw a reason to fight fire with fire."
She would continue to pile up victory after victory, which would
eventually earn her the 1996 PGWA Rookie of the Year honors.

Through all her hard work and dedication, Laurer became a
legitimate wrestling star and her future in the business was getting
brighter and brighter as each day and match went by. Not one to
rest on her laurels, the woman freshman wrestler of the year took
up karate and boxing and added these fighting skills to her already
awesome arsenal. She was not only turning herself into a better
wrestler, but she was also on course to becoming the ultimate fighting machine!

Now armed with the skills and confidence needed to succeed in
the grappling business, she started to take her career in her own
hands. She publicly challenged one of the WCW's female personalities, Madusa, to a match, but was turned down. It was lucky for
Madusa that the WCW had no interest in an all-female match,
because Laurer would have wiped the mat with her.

After having no success calling out other women to fight her,
she did what others deemed unthinkable and publicly challenged
other federations' top male talent to step between the ropes against
her. When no male stepped forward, she took advantage of a TV
appearance she was doing one night for an AIWF wrestling show
and reissued the challenge. One of the other guests, Bad Brad,
laughed at her dare, but it was Lee who would get the last chuckle
on this macho grappler.

When Joanie's female opponent was a no-show for her match
later that night, Bad Brad did the gentlemanly thing and offered his services as a replacement. Boy, was *that* a big mistake on
his part.

Lee not only jumped at the chance to showcase her skills; she jumped her male foe almost immediately and had her opponent dazed and confused during most of their contest. At one point during the match he ran out of the ring, only to return to use a different approach against his opponent. It's safe to say that on this night, Bad Brad lived up to his name against Lee and should have changed his ring moniker to "Scared" Brad. He, like so many before him, became a believer in her ring skills. But her biggest break was yet to come.

The now legitimate tough girl would get a call from one of her fellow Kowalski classmates, Hunter Hearst Helmsley, who wanted her to join him at the World Wrestling Federation. He was looking for a female bodyguard to escort him into the ring for his matches and she immediately came to mind. Helmsley didn't want someone who was going to be arm candy; he wanted someone who could watch his back. Lethal Laurer was about to get her just due and make it to the big time.

She first appeared on the WWF scene at ringside of HHH's matches and would cheer him on. But that would all change one night in Chattanooga, Tennessee at a WWF Final Four pay-per-view event. Helmsley would be battling Rocky Maivia that night for the Intercontinental strap, when Goldust and his valet/manager Marlena would interfere in the contest. Laurer immediately jumped out of her ringside seat and attacked Marlena in defense of HHH.

Helmsley hired her on the spot. On May 23, 1997, at WrestleMania, he introduced her as Chyna, his new valet/bodyguard. He was scheduled to take on Goldust, who was sure to be escorted to the ring by his other half, Marlena. The fans reacted positively to Hunter's new sidekick, and they enjoyed watching her go after Marlena and stick up for her man.

Chyna, who would eventually mix it up with the big boys like The Undertaker, "Stone Cold" Steve Austin and Goldust, was one of the founding members of the WWF gang D-Generation X. This would help her career tremendously, because she was now involved in story lines on a nightly basis.

The new WWF personality took advantage of every opportunity thrown her way by the federation. In 1999, she became the first woman wrestler to compete in both the King of the Ring tournament and the Royal Rumble. Although she didn't win either event, she proved to her male counterparts that she could hold her own. Later in the year, she would not only defeat a male wrestler in the ring, she would also steal his championship belt.

She won her first championship strap against Jeff Jarrett in October 1999 at a No Mercy event for the right to be called Intercontinental Champion. Chyna would hold onto the belt for almost two months until Chris Jericho came along and beat her on December 12 in Ft. Lauderdale, Florida. She was not only recognized by her peers as being successful, but she was also noticed by the fans, who voted her the 1999 Diva of the Year.

She started off the millennium right, as she would earn her second Intercontinental title in a match that took place in Miami on January 3, 2000. Although she had to share the belt with Chris Jericho because of a controversy that occurred between the two refs in the ring that night, she didn't care, because she could still add the federation gold to her expanding wrestling resume.

"The Ninth Wonder of the World," as she has been called, has left people wondering time and time again throughout her illustrious career, but now the only thing left to wonder is when she will become World Heavyweight Champion.

Goldberg

REAL NAME: William Scott Goldberg

HEIGHT: 6'3"

WEIGHT: 285 lbs.

BIRTHPLACE: Tulsa, Oklahoma

FINISHING MOVE: The Jackhammer

FAVORITE QUOTE: "Who's next?"

DID you ever go to the supermarket and purchase the less expensive, less glorified version of the product you wanted and came away liking it better than the more expensive, more hyped and more popular one? Well, this is kind of what happened several years ago when Goldberg first came onto the World Championship Wrestling scene.

Goldberg is the modern-day version of a no-frills wrestler who comes to the arena packaged only in his black trunks, black boots and a menacing scowl. He is not the type of wrestler who needs to work the crowd with the mic or one who has to be hyped up to find fame. What you see is what you get with him, and believe me, not many grapplers want to get what he's going to give them in the ring.

The bald wrestler first came onto the scene in 1997, when he took part in a mid-card fight with a seasoned veteran. His career just took off from there. The crowd started to get behind this rookie more and more as he was racking up victory after victory. What was ironic about this whole scenario was that the federation had big-time players like Hulk Hogan and Sting who weren't getting the cheers and reactions that this freshman was getting, and here Goldberg was making close to the league minimum while Hogan and company were making superstar money. It just goes to show that it's not what the outside of the box looks like that's important; it's more about what's inside the box that counts.

If you had to start from scratch and build a modern-day warrior for the ring, a so-called wrestling machine created solely for the purpose of winning matches in the least amount of time, you would have to look no further than Goldberg. Just photocopy the blueprints of his makeup and you'll have a seek-and-destroy weapon on your hands. The WCW now knows what they have in Goldberg after watching him work over the past three years. Proof of this fact can be found if you load the WCW's new video game, WCW Mayhem, into your computer and just watch the game's beginning promo.

Mayhem has a mode where the players can build their own wrestler to take on the WCW's best. In that mode, you can add your wrestler's characteristics, like height, weight, look, finishing move, and several other features. The opening promo has WCW officials building the ultimate wrestler, and what does the finished product come out looking like? You guessed it—Goldberg! As a matter of fact, the created wrestler comes to life before the officials are even done and starts tearing apart everything in sight à la Frankenstein; à la Monday Nitro!

Several years back, World Championship Wrestling had a character similar to Goldberg called "Stunning Steve" who wrestled in simple black trunks and black boots. The powers that be at the time fired him from the federation, claiming that pro wrestling had no room for someone who wrestled in such a plain outfit and who didn't say too much in the ring. Well, that "stunning" wrestler was Stone Cold Steve Austin, so you can bet that they won't make that same mistake again with Goldberg!

Goldberg was born William Scott Goldberg on December 27, 1966, in Tulsa, Oklahoma, to Dr. Jed Goldberg, an obstetrician, and his wife Ethel, a concert violinist who played with the Tulsa Symphony Orchestra. The youngest child of four, Bill was destined to be some kind of pro athlete, as he was rock-solid from an early age. At age sixteen, he lied about his age so he could get a job as a bouncer in a local bar. It worked because no one questioned his age, due to his immense size. While growing up, his first love was playing football and his second was his idol John Matuszak, the late-crazed Oakland Raiders' defensive lineman who terrorized his NFL opponents for many, many years.

Like Matuszak, Goldberg liked "living on the edge" and playing defense. In his spare time, he loved to fly acrobatic planes and gliders with his two brothers at home in Tulsa. He went to college at the University of Georgia, where he played football for the Bulldogs, and graduated with a degree in psychology.

The University of Georgia athletic director, Vince Dooley, who also coached Goldberg, remembers him as a soft-spoken guy who had a colorful personality and a nose for being around the ball. Of course he had a nose for being around the ball . . . Goldberg played nose tackle for four years while he was in college. "He was a relentless player," Dooley said.

The defensive captain, who wore number ninety-five, put up some great numbers for the Bulldogs in his career there from 1986 to 1989. He currently ranks eighth in total tackles (348), is tied for eighth in unassisted tackles (170), and stands at sixth in both tackle assists (178) and quarterback sacks (12). In order for him to put up such numbers, Dooley said he had to be around the play: "That means he had to be around the ball to do that." Goldberg set two school records as a defensive lineman. The first record was the 348 total career tackles, and the second was the 121 tackles he notched in his senior season.

His aggressive style of play earned him not only All-American honors from Football News and two-time All-Southwestern Conference status, it also garnered him the opportunity to be drafted by the Los Angeles Rams in the eleventh round of the 1990 NFL draft.

In his rookie season with the Rams, he roomed with current NFL all-pro defender Kevin Greene. It was a perfect match; not only did the two players share a love for playing on the defensive side of the ball, they also shared a love for pro wrestling. "Greene did a mean imitation of Hulk Hogan and we had something in common—we were both nuts about wrestling," Goldberg said.

Unfortunately for the rookie lineman, he wouldn't get to be Greene's roommate for much longer. As a matter of fact, he wouldn't even play a regular-season game for the Rams, since he was cut from the squad on two separate occasions.

In 1991, after being cut by the Rams, Goldberg found employment at an adult nightclub in Atlanta as a bouncer. While working there he ran into Diamond Dallas Page (DDP) and the two got to talking. One of the topics that came up was whether Goldberg would ever consider becoming a pro wrestler.

"I never even considered wrestling to be an option because I thought it was silly," Goldberg said. "There was no way I was going to go out in front of millions of people wearing nothing but my underwear."

But DDP tried to make him understand that he'd never be as big a personality in football as he would be in pro wrestling. Page was sure he'd be a success on the circuit and "I hadn't even known the guy ten minutes," DDP said.

But Goldberg passed on the suggestion, as he was still determined to play pro ball. He took his talents to the World League of American Football and signed on with the Sacramento Surge. Before he returned to the NFL, he would help the Surge from his nose tackle position win a WLAF championship over the Orlando Thunder.

He returned to the NFL in the fall of 1992 when the Atlanta Falcons came calling. Goldberg would play two seasons in Atlanta before his career was cut short by a serious abdominal injury. Although he was selected in the 1995 expansion draft by Carolina Panthers, he was never able to play another NFL game due to his injury.

With his pro football career now behind him, Goldberg had to find another job that could challenge his mind and body, but one that would make him happy. He took up personal weight training for a while and was making a good living. But there was still something missing.

One day while he was training at Main Event Fitness Center in Atlanta, he was approached by two of its owners, Steve Borden and Lawrence Pfohl. They offered him a job to work with them, but the job wasn't in their gym. It was in the WCW. You see, Borden and Pfohl may have been gym owners by day, but they were pro wrestlers by night—and pretty good ones, too! Steve Borden is known to wrestling fans all over as "Sting" and Pfohl is known as "The Total Package," Lex Luger.

They persuaded the young trainer to meet with WCW executive Eric Bischoff, since they saw not only a pro wrestler in the making, but a future wrestling star. He contacted his former teammate and roommate Kevin Greene, who had made his WCW ring debut only a year earlier in June 1996, for advice, and Greene gave him nothing but words of encouragement.

Goldberg agreed to give pro wrestling a shot, so he enlisted himself in the Power Plant, the WCW training facility for their up-and-coming pro wrestlers. He underwent six grueling months of training under Jody "The Assassin" Hamilton, where he learned his two trademark maneuvers, the spear and the jackhammer, along with several others, such as the corkscrew and the gorilla press.

Looking back, even though his days in the gym spent as a trainer didn't even compare to what he had endured under Hamilton in the Power Plant, Goldberg realized that it helped prepare him for what lay ahead. He was even fortunate enough to train with the late great Bruiser Brody, who would often frequent his workplace. He got a kick out of watching Brody pump iron, as he used to watch him take on opponents on Texas Championship Wrestling on

ESPN, and was amazed at the pro wrestler's size when he saw him in person.

"I really admired him," Goldberg said. "Here was this intimidating giant who never said anything. He just went in there, humiliated and kicked the hell out of his opponent, then left. I told myself that I wouldn't mind doing that, too." So Brody's tactics in and out of the ring would have a tremendous influence on Goldberg's career.

The rookie grappler's first TV appearance came in March 1997 while he was still training in the Power Plant. He would appear alongside Roddy Piper when the veteran wrestler was planning to recruit some young unknown wrestlers to form a team to go up against an nWo squad in a WCW event called Uncensored. The plan wound up falling through, because Piper used Ric Flair's Four Horsemen instead of Goldberg and the other young wrestlers.

But six months later, upon graduating from the Power Plant, Goldberg made his pro wrestling debut on a Monday Nitro event against a veteran mid-carder named Hugh Morrus. In what would be a sign of things to come, Goldberg dispatched his opponent almost before the match even started on that memorable night in September 1997. If you were watching from home and got up to answer the phone, went to take out the garbage or went to the kitchen for some soda and popcorn, you missed it!

Although it was considered just a mild upset, the fans were probably just as shocked as Morrus and the announcers were. That night's commentators, Tony Schiovani and Bobby "The Brain" Heenan didn't have much info on Goldberg. As a matter of fact, they didn't even know where he was born. They would comment that he's "from parts unknown," something that would stick with him for a while. When the match was over, Gene Okerlund tried to interview Goldberg, but he wasn't very successful. After one question, the night's victor just stared at Okerlund and then turned and walked off camera and backstage. He would prove to be a man of very few words. He was not a screamer or a bragger after matches. He would prove to be simply a winner.

"I don't like those typical screaming wrestler interviews and I don't want to do them," he said. "That used to be the norm, but it's changing. That's not my style.

"I'm a man of very few words," he would later say in a wrestling magazine interview. "I do my talking in the ring."

It was rare for a rookie to win his first match, but what was even more shocking and impressive was that the freshman grappler kept piling up the victories. The WCW was now in a bind. They had this young star on the rise and wanted to give him a push and ride his popularity, but how could they do this and not piss off the veterans, who were also getting paid a ton of money? They had big decisions to make and they knew that some toes and egos were going to be stepped on.

"They had no idea what to do with me," Goldberg would laugh and say later on in an interview when he looked back at his early success. "No idea. Do you remember where I used to be from? Parts unknown."

The WCW officials decided to ride the Tulsa Tornado, and their decision proved to be a smart one all around. Not only did Goldberg roll over everyone thrown his way, like a good tornado should, his ring presence was keeping the ratings up and the WCW was also rolling in the dough with their sales of Goldberg-related merchandise. According to a WCW source, over $400,000 worth of various Goldberg souvenirs were sold nationwide in September 1997 during his first month as a pro alone.

It didn't matter who stepped through the ropes against this mean Tulsa sensation; he would beat them, and in lightning-quick fashion. Some of his opponents who fell prey to his wrath in the beginning were The Barbarian, Renegade, Wrath, Scotty Riggs, Bobby Eaton, Stevie Ray and Steve "Mongo" McMichael.

McMichael was Goldberg's first true rival, as a matter of fact. The two ex-football players battled inside and outside the ring for a while, getting under each other's skin on several occasions. Mongo was personally trying to put an end to Goldberg's winning streak by interfering with his matches. Goldberg was stewing over the former Chicago Bears' antics and wanted to get revenge on his fellow grappler in the worst way. He got his revenge on McMichael at the 1997 Halloween Havoc, when he not only played hired gun to Mongo's wife Debra on that night, but interfered in McMichael's match and helped him lose.

The next wave of losers to dare step foot into the ring against Goldberg were Brad Armstrong, Dave Finlay, Lord Steven Regal and Ray Traylor. Then, on a Nitro broadcast, on April 20, 1998, things would only get better for the rock-solid wrestler. He would face the U.S. Heavyweight champion of the WCW, Raven, who agreed to put his belt on the line that night. The only stipulation of the contest was that the match would be played by Raven's rules. And his rules were: Anything goes!

Everyone thought that this would be bad news for Goldberg, because the minute Raven got into trouble his Flock would enter the ring to help save their leader. Well, this wasn't the case early on while Raven was getting the best of his opponent, but somewhere in the middle of the match Goldberg took over. He tossed his opponent around like a tackle dummy. And speaking of dummies, he would dispatch Raven's Flock one by one as they entered the ring.

Twice during the match, Goldberg swung Raven into the steel guardrail. After the second time, the beaten-up grappler tried to hit him with a chair, but would regret the tactic when Goldberg nailed him with a spear. With their leader in obvious trouble, Flock members Sick Boy and Kidman climbed into the ring to try and help, but their efforts were thwarted. Horace then tried to come to the rescue and hit Goldberg with a stop sign. This only seemed to make him madder, and he took his rage out on Flock member Grease, laying him out with a jackhammer.

While Goldberg was tending to the Flock, Raven tried to escape the match with both his health and belt still in good shape. But Raven was not that lucky or that popular, because the fans helped keep him from getting backstage, enabling Goldberg to capture him and toss him back into the ring.

Raven should have said "nevermore" before entering the ropes again, because he would pay dearly for his dirty tactics. The first order of business once they got back into the ring was for Goldberg to give him his second spear of the evening. As the crowd erupted, knowing what was coming next, Goldberg applied the jackhammer for the pin and the victory! He was now the new U.S. Heavyweight Champion of the federation.

Goldberg would successfully defend his title over the next few months against the likes of Mike Enos, Scott Norton, Saturn, Sick Boy, Glacier, La Parka and countless others. La Parka, as a matter of fact, paid dearly for stepping into the ring with Goldberg—the bald meanie tore up the Mexican grappler's knee. Hey, what's fair is fair . . . you wanna play, you have to be prepared to pay!

Around June 1998, Goldberg's record was closing in on one hundred wins and no losses. Could anyone dare challenge if the Tulsa tough guy was for real? Could anyone now doubt that he was main-event material? Well, certain vets still weren't happy with the new kid on the block, and they vowed to knock him off his high horse. Others wanted no part of him and did everything to avoid having to step into the ring with him. They feared that if they did enter, they might not be able to exit. But they were mistaken, because every arena had stretchers and paramedics present, so they would be able to leave the ring with no problem.

June 13, 1998 would be another important date in Goldberg's new career. It was just supposed to be a house show in Pittsburgh at the A. J. Palumbo Center, where he was scheduled to face Konnan. The Tulsa native would not only face and beat Konnan in thirty seconds on this memorable occasion, but more importantly he would challenge Sting and square off against the Wolfpac member. There would be some interference from other federation members (Kidman, Scotty Riggs and Barry Darsow), but once the two superstars cleared them from the ring, the match resumed.

Goldberg, in typical football player's fashion, tackled Sting and applied the jackhammer. Before you knew it, Goldberg had defeated one of the most well-respected wrestlers on the circuit. He had sent a message loud and clear to all the veterans on this night— beware, they could be next!

The nWo really went after Goldberg big time after he beat up on

Sting, but one by one they would also fall victim to the jackhammer and would become believers, like the unfortunate wrestlers before them.

Less than one month later, Goldberg would really leave his mark on the WCW. On July 6 in Atlanta, the city where he had played both college and professional ball, he would put his 106–0 record on the line before forty thousand screaming fans. Billed as the biggest Nitro ever, Goldberg wouldn't disappoint his hometown fans or himself, as he beat Scott Hall and Hulk Hogan to win the WCW Heavyweight Championship title and belt. The leader of the nWo, "Hollywood" Hogan, was now also a believer in the chiseled-out grappler. Many felt that this was sort of a handing over of the torch from a past great to a future great. But we would later find out that Hogan was not that gracious a loser.

Goldberg would hold onto the World Strap for four months and continue to add to his amazing unbeaten streak, while also successfully defending his title. Then on December 27, 1998, his first WCW Championship title reign and unbeaten streak would come to an end. He would face Kevin Nash at Starrcade in Washington, DC, in a nondisqualification match and lose his belt and the match when Nash was aided in his victory by outside help.

The first distraction for Goldberg was interference from both Disco Inferno and Bam Bam Bigelow. Then just when he thought he could concentrate on beating Nash, along came Scott Hall with a tazer gun. Hall shocked Goldberg and rendered him helpless with the tazer, allowing his good friend Nash to get the pin, win and championship belt! This loss would end Goldberg's unbeaten streak at an amazing 173 matches.

Surprisingly, Nash would demand a rematch, citing that he

wanted to beat Goldberg fair and square, without any controversy lingering over the match. Goldberg agreed to a rematch, which was to take place in Atlanta on January 4 in front of all his school-town folks. Well, a funny thing happened on the way to Georgia—Goldberg was "arrested" by the Atlanta police on charges of stalking one of the WCW female personalities, Miss Elizabeth, who was an ally of the nWo. Something fishy was definitely going on behind the scenes here.

When Goldberg didn't show, Nash challenged Hulk Hogan, who was supposedly present that night to announce his retirement. Hogan accepted and filled in for the absent Goldberg for a chance at another world title. The two went at it for the belt—well, sort of. During the course of the match, Nash rolled over and allowed Hogan to pin him and win back the belt he had lost to the Tulsa Tornado six months earlier. The fix was in! What a coincidence that just as Hogan won the strap, Goldberg was released from prison after Elizabeth dropped the charges. The young wrestler was humiliated.

But Goldberg took the incident in stride, awaiting his revenge and striking when his foes least expected. He would have many great battles after this incident in the months and year ahead. He would tussle with the likes of Scott Hall, Bam Bam Bigelow, Kevin Nash, Sting, Bret Hart and Sid Vicious. He would then add his third championship belt to his repertoire when he teamed with Bret "The Hitman" Hart to win the tag-team straps on December 7, 1999, in Madison, Wisconsin.

He has come so far in such a short period of time. His potential is unlimited in the wrestling business. Besides the wrestling-related magazines, Goldberg's goateed face has graced many famous publications. He has appeared on the cover of *Entertainment Weekly*, *TV Guide* and *POV*. He has also been featured in *People*, *Spin*, *Gear*, *Rolling Stone*, *Jerusalem Report*, *React Magazine*, the *New York Daily News*, the *New York Post*, and *USA Today*. But who knows how much longer he will be between the ropes; all signs point to his one day pursuing an acting career.

He made his acting debut on the *Love Boat* and made his big-screen debut last year with Jean-Claude Van Damme in *Universal Soldier II*. He has also made guest appearances on such TV shows as *The Tonight Show with Jay Leno*, *Live With Regis & Kathie Lee* and *The Dennis Miller Show*.

The six-foot-three, 285-pound Goldberg is not only a gifted athlete, but also a good role model, which nowadays seems hard to find. He's always taking time out to sign autographs and chat with his fans. He's deeply involved in many charities, including the Make-A-Wish Foundation, because he wants to help in any way he can. He knows that while his talent, a little luck and determination may have gotten him where he is today, whether he'll be around tomorrow ultimately lies in the hands of the fans. "I have a responsibility to the fans," he said. "It sends chills down my spine when they chant my name."

If Goldberg doesn't make it on the screen, he'll always have a place on the mat, because the fans won't become tired of chanting his name, that's for sure!

Bret Hart

REAL NAME: **Bret Hart**

HEIGHT: **5'11"**

WEIGHT: **235 lbs.**

BIRTHPLACE: **Calgary, Alberta**

FINISHING MOVE: **The Sharpshooter**

FAVORITE QUOTE: **"I'm the best there is, the best there was and the best there ever will be!"**

IN an industry full of good guys and bad guys, Bret "The Hitman" Hart has proven time and time again that not only is he one of wrestling's good guys in the ring, he can be looked on as a role model for the kids who tune in to watch him ply his trade.

Although Hart is not thrilled with what wrestling has become today, he would never turn his back on the young people who love the sport. He hates the fact that wrestling has become more about adult-related story lines and drama instead of the one-on-one battles in between the ropes. Because of these changes, he doesn't believe that this crude and violent form of entertainment is suitable for kids.

In one of his columns posted on his official Website (www. brethart.net), The Hitman had this to say about modern-day wrestling: "My kids don't watch wrestling. They don't want to. And if they did want to, as a parent, I wouldn't let them. I've said [it] before and I'll say it again, wrestling is not for kids anymore.

"I still take being a positive role model for kids very seriously, and I even enjoy the responsibility that goes along with it, but now I'm finding other ways to do it outside of wrestling."

Even though Hart has frowned upon the industry of late, it can't take away from what he's accomplished in the professional wrestling ring during his career. He is not only the holder of seven world heavyweight titles, but he also earned the nicknames "The Hitman" and "The Excellence of Execution" by being one of the best technical wrestlers and fiercest brawlers in the game.

Born in Calgary, Alberta, on July 7, 1957, this Canadian native was destined to become a pro grappler. His father, Stu Hart, was not only a Hall of Fame wrestler in his time, but he also ran a wrestling school called The Dungeon.

The Hart family, like the Von Erichs, is definitely a wrestling family through and through. Not only did Stu, sons Bret, Keith, Bruce, Smith and the late Owen Hart earn their paychecks in the business, but two of Stu's sons-in-law, Jim "The Anvil" Neidhart and Davey Boy Smith, are also pro wrestlers. Even his daughters Diana and Ellie caught the wrestling bug and took part in a grappling gig with Stampede Wrestling.

Stu once said in an interview that he met his wife, Helen, at ringside. One night he was thrown from the ring during one of his bouts, and he landed right on the lap of his beautiful future wife. That was truly a match made in wrestling heaven.

The Dungeon was literally located right under Bret's nose—in his basement—and while the elder Hart would hold class, his sons would sit in and watch. Stu's Dungeon was so well-known and well-respected in the industry that wanna-be wrestlers such as "Rowdy" Roddy Piper, Chris Benoit, Jim Neidhart, Davey Boy Smith, Chris Jericho and countless others came from all over just to learn the trade from this master.

When he was old enough, Bret even became one of his dad's students and would go on to dominate the Canadian amateur ranks during his teens. He would capture city and provincial championships in three different weight classes while he was still a student at Ernest Manning High School in Calgary. From the amateurs, he would move on into his dad's federation, Stampede Wrestling, and would get his feet wet in the small Canadian promotion, making his pro debut against Dennis Stamp at the age of twenty-one.

He would win his first singles title only two years later, as he captured the Stampede British Commonwealth Mid-Heavyweight title in September 1978 against Norman Frederich Charles III. In that same year, he would team with his brother Smith and garner his first tag belt of his young career, as the Hart siblings captured the WWC tag straps from the Castillo Brothers.

The Calgary grappler would go on to win another seven titles in his career with Stampede—he would capture the Mid-Heavyweight title one more time (in April 1979 against The Dynamite Kid), and the North American Heavyweight title six times, the first in 1980 against his nemesis Leo Burke and the last in 1983 against Burke.

After Stampede, he would step between the ropes of several independent federations like the American Wrestling Association and the National Wrestling Alliance to further sharpen his skills. Not limiting his skills to the States, Bret would also try wrestling on the Japanese circuit, where he not only found success, but also some awesome competition.

But in 1984, he received the call he had been waiting for all his life—the World Wrestling Federation wanted his services. He entered the federation as a babyface, but that quickly changed when he was paired with his brother-in-law Jim "The Anvil" Neidhart. The two would stir up some controversy as The Hart Foundation along with their colorful manager Jimmy "The Mouth of the South" Hart (no relation).

At this time, Neidhart and Bret would start a vicious feud with the British Bulldogs (Davey Boy Smith and Dynamite Kid). This feud had all the makings of a soap opera, as Bret was not only paired with one of his brothers-in-law; he was also battling against another in-law, Smith. To make things even more interesting, Dynamite was one of his rivals from his Stampede days.

"The Hitman" and "The Anvil" would defeat the Bulldogs and keep the tag-team title in the family. They copped the straps from the duo on January 26, 1987, in Tampa, Florida. In typical bad-guy fashion, they not only double-teamed their brother-in-law Davey Boy, they also got some assistance from a corrupt ref named Danny Davis.

The duo held onto the belts for nine months until the Strike Force came along and took their title away on October 27, 1987, in

"Can you smell what The Rock has cooking, *jabroni*?"

J&E Sports Photography

Steve Austin poses with a couple of young fans.

Pics Pix

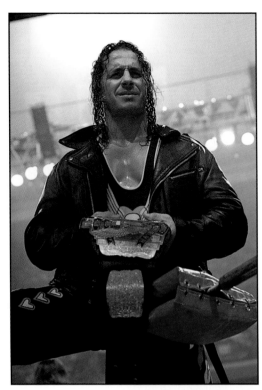

Bret Hart proudly displays
his World Heavyweight
Championship Belt.

R. Grabowski

Goldberg puts a
headlock on
The Hitman.

R. Grabowski

"Thou shall not mess with
D-Von Dudley!"

J&E Sports Photography

Jeff Hardy plans
The Hardy Boyz's next
move—will it be the Senton
Bomb or Twist of Fate?

J&E Sports Photography

An opponent's worst nightmare—
here comes the monstrous Big Show!

R. Grabowski

Kane holds X-Pac's hand up in victory—or maybe not!

J&E Sports Photography

Hulk Hogan makes a grand entrance.

R. Grabowski

Two legends of the ring, Hogan and Goldberg, go at it!

R. Grabowski

"Big Sexy" Kevin Nash explodes on Nitro!

R. Grabowski

Syracuse, New York. The Hart Foundation would again capture the prestigious tag title, but not until three years later, on August 27, 1990. They defeated the Demolition team for the belts, a reign which would last only three months.

In 1991, The Hitman resumed his singles career, and almost immediately he was in contention for the Intercontinental title, which was held by Curt "Mr. Perfect" Hennig at the time. When Hennig granted Hart a shot at him and the title, Hart jumped all over the opportunity and his foe. He beat "Mr. Perfect" at Summer-Slam in New York on August 26, 1991, in a memorable match where he debuted his finishing hold "The Sharpshooter," a variation of the ever-famous Boston crab hold.

He held onto this title for five months before he would lose the strap to the Mountie (Jacques Rougeau) on January 17, 1992, in Springfield, Massachusetts. But he wasn't without the belt for long; he regained the Intercontinental title in April against "Rowdy" Roddy Piper in Indianapolis, Indiana. In his second tour of duty as IC champ, Bret was to embark on some of his greatest matches and rivalries in his WWF career. He met up and started a long-lasting feud with "The Heartbreak Kid" Shawn Michaels and would engage in one of the best contests of his career with his bro-in-law Davey Boy Smith.

On August 29, 1992, at SummerSlam in London's Wembley Stadium, in front of his nation's fans, Davey Boy would square off against Hart with not only the Intercontinental title on the line, but family and hometown pride as well. They would treat eighty thousand of England's faithful to one of the best matches of the year, as Smith and The Hitman used every technique they knew in the action-packed match which lasted almost thirty minutes. When the grueling contest was over, Smith emerged victorious, pinning Hart for the win and ending The Hitman's four-month run as champ.

But The Excellence of Execution wouldn't be without gold for long, for Hart would win the most prestigious belt in the WWF—the World Heavyweight title—less than two months after his loss to Smith.

In October 1992, Hart won his first of five world titles in front of his country's fans in Saskatoon, Saskatchewan, Canada, against the ever-popular Ric Flair. This upset was only the beginning of a great singles career—he would now do battle with all the federation stars, and one by one they would fall victim to his lethal sharp-shooter. His reign would last only six months, but not to worry—four more WWF heavyweight belts were in the cards for this super grappler. A 1993 King of the Ring title would also come his way before he would get back on top of the WWF's championship mountain.

Less than two years after his first heavyweight belt, he would recapture the distinguished strap in world-class fashion in front of twenty thousand crazed fans in New York's Madison Square Garden at WrestleMania X. His opponent, Yokazuna, was a genuine heavyweight, tipping the scales at six hundred pounds. Needless to say, the 230-pound Hart went in as a "heavy" underdog.

His chances appeared even worse going into the championship match that day, because he had also squared-off against his younger brother Owen earlier in the event and lost. During the press conference after WrestleMania X, the elder Hart had this to say about going against his brother that day: "I didn't want it to occupy my mind going into the last match [against Yokazuna]," Bret explained. "But the fact is that my brother Owen is a good wrestler."

The family feud had been building up all year, with Owen continuously calling out his brother to wrestle him in the ring. When they finally clashed on this day in May, the crowd would not be disappointed, as the brothers showed off what they had learned from their father years ago in the comfort of their own basement.

As the younger Hart relished in his win over his brother, Bret was just glad to have the match over with. He had been trying to avoid the collision course that they were on, but Owen seemed hellbent on grappling with his own family member in the ring.

"I've been reluctant all along [to wrestle my brother]," Hart explained at the time. "I don't feel comfortable wrestling my own brother." But when asked if he thought Owen was the better grappler of the two, he confidently replied: "Owen is the kind of wrestler who could beat me one time out of ten."

Not happy with his brother's words, Owen continued the brotherly ring feud and tried to turn everyone against Bret. Owen reached out to their brother-in-law Jim "The Anvil" Neidhart, Bret's former tag-team partner, to help him bring down his brother's career. The two grapplers plotted and caused The Hitman to lose one of his matches against Kevin Nash, then known as Diesel to the WWF fans.

Determined to end his brother's title reign, Owen then turned his attention to convincing former WWF champion and wrestling legend Bob Backlund to help him with his quest. Backlund would square off against Bret in the 1994 Survivor Series in a submission match, where each wrestler handpicks a partner to accompany him into the ring and literally throws in the towel if he wants to submit to his opponent.

The choices for both men on this night in San Antonio, Texas, were obvious. Backlund chose Owen, while Bret would choose his brother-in-law Davey Boy Smith. The match would be full of crazy twists and turns, but the ending was the most bizarre. With Backlund having Bret in a vicious submission hold and his partner incapacitated, Owen reached out to his mom, who was sitting at ringside to throw in the towel to help save her son. Not wanting to see her son hurt, Mrs. Hart complied with Owen's plea and tossed in the towel, causing The Hitman to lose even though he never submitted.

Furious with his brother and the outcome in the Lone Star State, Hart was now more determined than ever to get back his championship belt. Backlund would lose his belt three days later to Diesel in New York, and the seven-foot wrestler would hold onto the belt for almost a year until the Royal Rumble in 1995.

On November 29, 1995, Bret Hart was ready to reclaim his title from Diesel at the Rumble, but there was one problem—well, maybe two—both Owen and Backlund were going to be present and neither wanted to see The Hitman regain the title.

The Bret/Diesel contest was full of outside interference, which caused Hart to lose his temper and pummel anyone in his way. Two of the victims were of the sweet revenge type, as Bret nailed his brother Owen and his sidekick Backlund. The night would end with Bret back on top of the WWF, as he also would defeat Diesel in the process.

In the course of winning his third title, Bret became "The Marked Man" instead of "The Hitman," because he would become involved in several feuds with the likes of The Undertaker, Shawn Michaels, Diesel and Davey Boy Smith. Everyone now wanted a piece of the WWF's number one guy, but Bret didn't mind—if the matches were fair and square—as it came with the championship territory. But his matches would increasingly involve some kind of outside interference, and Hart was not a happy camper.

One of these royal screw jobs occurred at WrestleMania XII on March 31, 1996, where Hart was to take on Shawn Michaels in a title-defense match. The two stars would clash for sixty solid minutes, with the match supposedly ending in a draw and Hart retaining his belt. But after Bret had already left the ring, he was ordered to go back by the WWF's president at the time, Gorilla Monsoon, to take part in an overtime session to determine a winner. The added time resulted in Bret losing the belt to Michaels, which made him sour against the federation.

He would go on to win the title back in Knoxville, Tennessee, on February 16, 1997, in a Final Four match, where he would eventually defeat The Undertaker and take home his fourth Heavyweight belt. This title reign was to be his shortest and one of the most frustrating of his career, as it would last only one day.

The next night, Sycho Sid would take away the strap from Hart with the aid of an outsider. Steve Austin would interfere in the tilt and cause Hart to lose to the crazy wrestler, prompting The Hitman to get into a microphone shouting match with his boss Vince McMahon.

Hart didn't take very kindly to Austin interfering in his title match, so when WrestleMania XIII rolled around, The Hitman was all ready to heat things up with Stone Cold. The two battled in an awesome match, with Austin and Hart pummeling each other unmercifully both inside and outside the ropes. The two even smashed each other with any foreign object that was lying around. This would be one of Hart's last great victories in the federation that he represented so well over the years.

He would win his fifth and final WWF title against The Under-taker on August 3, 1997, in a match at the Meadowlands in East Rutherford, New Jersey. This three-month reign led to a bitter feud with Vince McMahon, which ultimately caused The Hitman to leave the WWF.

. The scene of the crime would be in Canada—Hart's home-land—on November 9, 1997. He squared off against his arch-rival Shawn Michaels for the last time in what was to become one of the biggest wrestling conspiracies ever. The supposedly worked-out sce-nario was for Hart to lose the belt to Michaels, since he was leaving the federation once his contract expired in December. But it wasn't supposed to be on this night in Montreal. It was supposed to hap-pen the following evening at another WWF event.

But Vince had other plans for the Canadian grappler. He knew Hart was leaving for the WCW, so he plotted to turn the tables on the wrestler one last time. The moment Michaels would get Bret in his own sharpshooter hold, McMahon would order the bell to be rung, ending the contest and giving Michaels the belt and win.

When this took place, Michaels rushed out of the ring with the belt in his hand and a confused look on his face. Hart first took out his frustrations on the TV monitors at ringside. Then he spat in the face of McMahon on his way backstage. While backstage, he confronted Michaels as to why he had plotted against him, and The Heartbreak Kid immediately told Hart he had no idea about what had taken place out there. Michaels swore to the Calgary native that he had no idea about McMahon's plan to have Hart lose his title that night.

The Hitman then lived up to his name, as he then sought out his boss and made him the next person on his "hit" list. Not in the mood for small talk, Hart would knock McMahon senseless, thus exiting the WWF with a bang.

Hart would move to the WCW, where he would make his debut at a federation pay-per-view entitled Souled Out. Bret would win his debut match over fellow veteran wrestler Ric Flair when he nailed him with one of his lethal sharpshooters, thus beginning a new chapter in his wrestling career.

He would establish himself as one of the federation's best by winning first their U.S. title three times and then the WCW's highest prize, the Heavyweight Championship, twice. His first WCW world title would be won on November 21, 1999, in front of his native country's people in Toronto. The WCW grappler would then have a busy month in December. He would not only vacate his title due to a controversial title-defense match against Goldberg, but would also team up with the bald behemoth on December 7 to win the tag-team title in Madison, Wisconsin. Then at the end of the month, he would win the WCW top prize for the second time in his career.

Bret Hart is as much a star outside the ring as he is inside. He not only writes a weekly column, which is often accompanied by one of his unique cartoons, for his hometown newspaper *The Calgary Sun*, but he has also appeared as himself in several TV programs including *Mad TV*, *The Simpsons* and *Honey I Shrunk the Kids*. He also made his character-acting debut on TV in *Lonesome Dove: The Series*, where he was to make one guest star appearance, but his performance was so well-received that he was invited back for six more episodes. Eventually the producers asked him back as a regular for the following season. His face has also been spotted on famous entertainment shows like *Lifestyles of the Rich and Famous*, *Live With Regis & Kathie Lee* and *Dini Petty*.

The Excellence of Execution was also a hit in an award-winning documentary entitled *Hitman Hart: Wrestling with Shadows*, which chronicles this champion wrestler's youth and the rise and fall of his WWF career. Hart is also a champion to children's causes like the Special Olympics. He regularly visits schools and hospitals so he can get his positive messages across to the kids of the world. His support of these children and his gracious acceptance of being a role model to them makes him an even greater champion away from the ring than inside the ropes.

Hulk Hogan

REAL NAME: **Terry Bollea**

HEIGHT: **6'8"**

WEIGHT: **275 lbs.**

BIRTHPLACE: **Augusta, Georgia**

FINISHING MOVE: **The Leg Drop**

FAVORITE QUOTE: **"What are you gonna do when these twenty-four-inch pythons run wild on you?"**

IT takes a very rare athlete to come along and change the way a professional sport is either played or perceived. In the early 1900s, Babe Ruth stepped up to the plate and almost single-handedly changed the way baseball was played. Ditto Michael Jordan's impact on modern-day basketball. Hulk Hogan can also be placed on that special list. He came onto the pro wrestling scene in the 1980s and took the sport where it never had been before.

Vince McMahon Jr., who hand-picked the Hulkster to lead his federation, truly believed that in 1991 Hogan's stamp on wrestling was well beyond Ruthian proportions. "I don't know anything that could compare with Hulk at the moment. I think he's gone beyond Babe Ruth."

While Ruth and Jordan impacted their various sports mostly with their God-given skills, Hogan revolutionized wrestling mostly with his personality. He had the ability to put his finger on the pulse of the crowd the moment he walked into an arena and ride the wave straight into their hearts.

He redefined wrestling in such a way that people were no longer embarrassed to admit they were fans. As a matter of fact, he made the wrestling arena the "in" place to be. At one time, WWF event tickets became so hot that even celebrities had to wait on line to find out if they were going to be able to get in.

Many wonder why Hogan had such an impact on the popularity of wrestling, but one of the common reasons always seems to be his showmanship. Hogan always seems to put on a great show for his audience, and you can tell by their responses that they appreciate his efforts. No matter who stands opposite the blond bomber in the ring, he always plays to the crowd, letting them know that he hasn't forgotten them.

But being the modest guy that he is, the Hulk takes no credit for changing the way wrestling is viewed today. He places the credit for its popularity elsewhere: "We quit insulting people's intelligence," he said. "It [wrestling] went from being a sport to being sports entertainment."

And that's exactly why Hogan was able to carry wrestling on his muscular back. He is definitely an entertainer first and a wrestler second. Although he stands an imposing six-foot-eight and tips the scales at 275, he doesn't have the greatest mat skills in the business. As a matter of fact, some will argue that his technical skills and ring techniques are nowhere to be found—but that never stopped the determined grappler from reaching the pinnacle of his industry.

Born in Augusta, Georgia, Hogan didn't attend his first wrestling match until his family moved to Tampa, Florida, years later. His dad, Peter, took him to a card at the Tampa Armory and immediately the little Hulkster fell in love with what he saw.

The future wrestler came into this world as Terry Bollea on August 11, 1953, to a construction foreman and his dance-teaching wife, Ruth. Bollea was destined to be somewhere in the spotlight as an adult, just like he was as a child. He was breaking scales and heads from early on—he weighed in at 195 pounds at the age of twelve and was constantly getting into fights at school.

When he entered high school, Terry's parents thought he would calm down a bit and take some of his aggression out on his opponents when he joined the school's wrestling team. But this wouldn't be the case for Bollea. Again, he would find himself in trouble with his hands and would be sent to reform school, the Florida Sheriff's Boy's Ranch, for street fighting at the age of fourteen.

Determined to change his life for the better, Bollea would eventually graduate high school and enter college. He studied at both the Hillsborough Community College and the University of South Florida, earning a degree in business. Although he was proud of his degree, deep down he knew his career wasn't in business, but in pro sports—wrestling, to be exact! Bollea wasn't a suit-and-tie type of guy. He would much rather be wearing a pair of wrestling trunks and boots if he had the choice.

Upon graduating, Bollea held several different jobs. He played bass for a rock band in Southern Florida and also worked in the scorching heat on the docks. But in his spare time, he sweated in a different way, as he hit the weights and tried out for any wrestling organization that would give him a shot. As a matter of fact, he gave new meaning to "trying to break into the business" as he literally broke his leg during a wrestling tryout for a regional federation.

Still determined to make it in the sport, Bollea constantly attended all events in his area, hoping that one day he would be noticed. His dream would come true one night while he was attending a card in Miami and was spotted by two WWF wrestlers who were taking part in that night's event.

Jack and Jerry Brisco noticed Bollea at ringside during their event and approached him afterward and asked him if he ever thought about pursuing a career in pro wrestling. Well, without hesitation, the future grappler answered: "I've wanted to be one all my life!"

He trained under the tutelage of the Briscos for a couple of months and then hit the mat scene in the sunny state as "The Super Destroyer." To get his feet wet, he toured the South and wrestled for regional outfits, where he started not only to learn his trade, but also to work the crowd. "I guess Terry gets his showmanship from me," his mom, Ruth, would say in an interview she did with *People* magazine in 1991.

He began to find steady work from the indies and make a name for himself in the process. And speaking of names, he stepped through the ropes as many different ones in the early stages of his career. At one time or another he was listed on a card somewhere not only as "The Super Destroyer," but also as "Sterling Golden" or "Terry Boulder." But no matter the name, the fans were beginning to recognize his talents and he had the crowds in a frenzy even this early in his career.

One promoter—the late Roy Shire—knew Bollea was destined to be someone special in the industry: "I could see the guy had great talent and abilities. He was big, particularly for the times, and young. I just don't think he knew exactly what he wanted to do or how to really make it to the big time in wrestling," he said at the time. "But I knew he could be a great superstar if he wanted. Although he wasn't quite as husky and so well muscled, at the time, he reminded me a bit of when I first saw and flew in Superstar Billy Graham. I told myself this guy had a great future if he worked it right."

Jerry Brisco seemed to agree with Shire's sentiments. "By the time he got into the ring, he was getting a standing ovation," Brisco explained. "Nobody had a clue who this was, but they were cheering him like he was already a superstar."

While he might have been getting the superstar's greeting, Bollea was not making superstar cash. As a matter of fact, he was barely getting by on what he was being paid. His checks at the end of the week would read an unimpressive $125, but he wasn't complaining, since he was being paid to do what he loved. The eager wrestler continued to ply his trade, knowing that as long as he was working in the biz, his big break would eventually come along.

Bollea was right. In 1979, while he was working for Verne Gagne in the AWA, he was discovered and recruited by none other than the owner of the WWF, Vince McMahon Sr. The owner immediately dubbed his new recruit "Terry Hogan," an Irish villain.

He wrestled as the Irish villain for a while, where his evil character's traits would help him later in his career, but the bad guy image was soon dumped for a heroic one. Bollea's character would now lose the Terry part of his name and it would be replaced by Hulk, a takeoff from the popular television show *The Incredible Hulk*.

He explained, "When I first started wrestling, the wrestling world was very territorial. They had Italian wrestlers, and they had Native Americans and they had wrestlers for the Polish people. They said [to me], 'You should be Hogan. Yeah,' they said, 'you should be Hulk Hogan.' "

Little did anyone know that they had just named a legend.

Along with the new image and name came a new manager, Freddie Blassie. Blassie seemed to be no help to his new grappler, at least when it came to winning those early matches—Hogan was beaten regularly from the top names in the business at the time, such as Superstar Billy Graham and Bob Backlund. But all this would change over time as the Hulkster started to stir things up in the federation little by little.

Another break came for the now pro wrestler in 1982. Sylvester Stallone came calling and cast the WWF grappler in his new movie *Rocky III*. Hogan played—what else?—a professional wrestler, Thunderlips, who would take on Rocky in a charity bout in the film. This role would leave a lasting impression on the audience, because in his memorable scene, not only did Hogan tower over Stallone in the ring, but he picked up the movie-star boxer over his head and launched him out of the ring into the crowd. This scene launched his wrestling career, and started a new era in the wrestling world.

Speaking of starting a new era, in that same year, Vince McMahon Jr. purchased the Capitol Wrestling Corporation from his father and also took over control of the WWF. When it came time for the new boss to choose the wrestler around whom he wanted to build his franchise, he looked over his roster at the time and decided to go with Hulk Hogan.

A year later, in June 1983, Hogan won his first championship belt, but surprisingly it wasn't with McMahon's federation. It was in Japan, where he beat Antonio Inoki in the finals of a tournament that determined the first-ever IWGP champ. (Later on in his career, Hogan admitted that this belt was the most important title in his career, since he won it strictly because of his wrestling skills and without the aid of his image.)

Under the direction of McMahon Jr., "Hulkamania" began to run wild. The first measuring stick of Hulk's popularity came in 1984 when he would win his first title in America. Hogan faced the Iron Sheik on January 23 and pinned him for his first WWF World Heavyweight title. From here on out, Hogan took hold of the wrestling world.

Dressed in his yellow and red battle gear, he would come out each week and preach to the young children across the world, now dubbed as his little "Hulkamaniacs," to "say your prayers, take your vitamins, drink your milk, and believe in yourself." He was quickly becoming a modern-day superhero whom the kids could look up to.

But wherever there's a hero, you can bet your bottom dollar that there's also a villain. At that time, Hogan's main foe was "Rowdy" Roddy Piper. Piper was the guy the fans loved to hate. In 1984 and 1985, he not only knew how to press Hogan's buttons, but also those of his most loyal fans. The boos for Piper were sometimes louder than the cheers for Hogan. It was the perfect good guy versus bad guy story line.

This would be a big year for Hogan, Piper and the rest of the wrestling world. The sport reached heights it had never seen before, and the Hulkster was the main reason for its popularity. Hulk Hogan would become a household name not only to wrestling fans, but worldwide. He would also introduce the world to the Rock 'n' Wrestling connection, where he would include performers from other forms of entertainment in wrestling story lines.

Two of the first entertainers to climb on board and enter the crazy world of wrestling were Mr. T and Cyndi Lauper, who participated in a wrestling event on February 18, 1985. The two stars immediately drew national attention and media coverage to their roles in the WWF affair. MTV even chose to air this card, The War to Settle the Score, live from Madison Square Garden in New York, for which they received not only good ratings, but also good responses from their viewers.

The next WWF event that Hogan would participate in would really put wrestling on the map. On March 31, 1985, the World Wrestling Federation and Hulk Hogan introduced the world to the Super Bowl of wrestling, WrestleMania. The event, where Muhammad Ali appeared as a guest referee, was only available through closed-circuit TV, yet still drew an audience of more than four hundred thousand people from across the country.

This was only the beginning for Hulk and the WWF. One of the best indicators of Hogan's legitimacy and popularity was his cover appearance on the April 29 issue of *Sports Illustrated*. This not only proved that wrestling was on top of the sports world at the time, but more important, that people in the industry were taking notice. That 1985 issue would also go on to be the magazine's best regular-selling issue of the year, besides the swimsuit issue.

Hogan was also responsible for helping bring wrestling back to network TV, as the WWF signed a deal with NBC to air a late-night wrestling program entitled *Saturday Night's Main Event*. The show, debuting in May 1985, was yet another success for Hogan and the federation.

The rest of the eighties saw many grapplers try to dethrone Hogan as the most popular wrestler in the WWF, but none ever came close. As a matter of fact, one of Hogan's greatest moments in between the ropes happened in 1987 at WrestleMania III—and "the Hulkster" couldn't have picked a better time or place to pull off the impossible.

In front of ninety-three thousand screaming WrestleManiacs (an attendance record for an indoor event) at the Pontiac Silverdome, Hulk Hogan not only pinned the legendary Andre the Giant and stripped him of his championship title, but more impressively, he picked up his seven-foot-four, 500-pound opponent and bodyslammed him to the canvas.

He won and lost the WWF World Heavyweight strap five times in his career with the federation, and through it all he acted like a champion. In his time in the WWF, Hogan squared off against some of wrestling's most popular personalities. He went head-to-head with Ric Flair, Randy "Macho Man" Savage, The Ultimate Warrior, Sgt. Slaughter, Razor Ramon, Big Boss Man, Sid Vicious, Jake "The Snake" Roberts, The Undertaker and countless others.

He not only got to wrestle some of the greatest athletes in the business at the time, he was also able to travel to some of the greatest cities in the world and show them what pro wrestling was really all about. The world's most famous grappler touched down in cities such as Los Angeles, Chicago, New York, San Francisco, Las Vegas, Houston, London, Paris, Berlin, Tokyo, Venice, Madrid and Rio de Janeiro.

With Hogan's ever-increasing popularity came an enormous

amount of interviews and personal appearance requests, which he tried to fulfill as best as his wrestling schedule would allow. Hogan became one of the first wrestlers to regularly appear on hit TV shows such as the *Tonight Show*, *Saturday Night Live*, *Late Night with David Letterman*, and *Live With Regis & Kathie Lee*. His mug would also grace the front covers of such publications as *TV Guide* and *USA Today*, as well as *Sports Illustrated*. These accomplishments alone left the WWF wrestler in a class by himself in the eighties.

But the nineties didn't start off too well for the WWF grappler. For the first time, a major controversy hit Hogan, and it hit like no other opponent ever did! Accusations of steroid abuse by Hogan and other popular wrestling personalities were under investigation by federal authorities, and for the first time the Hulkster's reign seemed threatened. Many felt that Hogan's career could be over if he was found guilty of using the physique-enhancing drugs, because throughout his career he had preached to his fans about living a clean, drug-free life.

When Hogan was forced to testify as a witness and admitted in open court that he had used steroids, it looked like it was the beginning of the end for the popular grappler. But Hogan once again beat the odds and, despite his testimony, his popularity remained intact.

He would go back to the WWF for a short while, and then he would take a hiatus from the sport and concentrate on his acting career. Although he appeared in several films and starred in his own action/adventure TV series, *Thunder in Paradise*, he still longed for the action in the ring.

"I was sitting in those trailers for twelve hours a day going,

'What am I doing here? I can still wrestle. I'm not that old,' "
Hogan explained.

On June 11, 1994, almost a year to the day of his last WWF
match, Ted Turner phoned Hulk and asked him to be a part of his
wrestling organization, World Championship Wrestling, which was
floundering at the time. Hogan almost immediately said yes and
signed on the dotted line, but many were questioning whether he
was past his prime and whether or not he could still create heat and
interest.

Never one to be bothered by obstacles, Hogan entered the
WCW and quickly proved his critics wrong. In typical Hogan fashion, he had a successful federation debut against the reigning champion Ric Flair. The only thing that was different this time around
was the fans' reaction.

The "Hulkamaniacs" had turned into maniacs for real, and
booed their longtime hero instead of cheering him. The legendary
wrestler was not only confused by their reaction; he was also angry
and bitter. Hogan decided to take matters into his own hands and
do the unthinkable—the good guy was about to turn heel!

And he was also about to change his ever-so-famous ring-name
to "Hollywood" Hogan, in reference to his acting career.

"Many people who have supported and followed me throughout the years wonder why did I change," he said. "What's with this
new 'Hollywood' Hulk attitude? Well, I guess you can say, brother,
that it took me many years to realize this, but I've finally come to
the conclusion that like the old saying, 'nice guys finish last.' I'm
tired of being the nice guy!"

Hogan even went a step further and joined the New World
Order (nWo), with other badass dudes such as Kevin Nash, Scott

Hall and Scott Steiner. The gang terrorized the federation for quite some time and at one time even almost took control of the WCW.

Whether Turner liked it or not, the fact that Hogan stirred up controversy within his new organization not only made for great wrestling and story lines, it more importantly put the WCW back into competition with the WWF.

"My colleagues and I, brother, have created the greatest league ever, and we're going to take the nWo to the highest levels," he stated. "Just look at us, [we're] the biggest, maddest, toughest wrestlers anywhere. We are the elite; the cream of the crop. No one can deny us and if you have any brains you'll join us if we offer. [But] that is only if we offer."

In his move from the WWF to the WCW, the future Hall of Famer proved to everyone in the wrestling world that he still had what it takes to be on top, since he held their heavyweight title on six different occasions. As for how much more time he will spend in the industry, no one knows for sure.

He has a lovely wife named Linda and a family to go home to in sunny Florida if he wants to live the good life and retire, but he also has the option to take up acting again. There have been rumors of Hogan one day running for president, given that his former foe Jesse Ventura became governor of Minnesota. Will he run for the ultimate office? It's hard to say, but never bet against the Hulkster, because you'll have to decide what to do if his twenty-four-inch pythons come down on you!

Chris Jericho

REAL NAME: Chris Irvine

HEIGHT: 6'0"

WEIGHT: 231 lbs.

BIRTHPLACE: Long Island, New York

FINISHING MOVE: The Walls of Jericho

FAVORITE QUOTE: "All hail the Ayatol-lah of rock 'n' roll-a!"

WHEN the year 2000 was making its way upon us, everyone in the civilized world worried about the Y2K problem, but their worries were for naught because 1999 turned into 2000 without a hitch. The wrestling world wasn't so lucky, especially all the grapplers in the WWF who were hearing rumors about a Y2J problem—namely, Chris Jericho—coming to their federation. The monsters of the ring were worried that this up-and-coming wrestler might be making his way into their backyard and would try to steal some of their glory.

Well, on August 19, 1999, their worst nightmare came true

when Jericho made his debut in a Chicago *RAW* event in the All-state Arena. The self-proclaimed savior of the federation made a most memorable entrance not only by coming into the ring in rock star-like fashion with loud blaring music and a pyrotechnic show, but by also engaging in a sparring match with one of the league's most prominent stars, The Rock. Although the sparring match was verbal rather than physical, the "millennium man" more than held his own against The Rock, who is known to be a master on the mic. The new kid on the block had spoken, and was definitely heard!

Jericho made his way into many families' homes on that unforgettable evening, and more important, he enlisted many new Jericoholics to his already uncountable list. His "Breaking Down the Walls" entrance music has now become one of the most recognizable and popular themes in the sports entertainment business, and he's only just begun.

"I see complete world domination for 'Y2J' in the federation," he recently claimed in an interview with *RAW* magazine, "because there's nobody who can stop me from doing that. There is a lot of great talent here and I want to fit in with everybody. I'm looking forward to having a long and illustrious career here and conquering every superstar to prove that 'Y2J' definitely will save the World Wrestling Federation."

Those are big words from a guy who only stands six feet tall and climbs into the ring with coworkers who average six-foot five, but you're not talking about any ordinary wrestler here. Jericho was not only born in rough and tough New York, he is also the son of a former New York Ranger hockey player, Ted Irvine, who happened to be his team's enforcer during his career. So you can honestly call him a chip off the old block—both father and son wouldn't think twice about chipping blocks off anyone who stood in their way.

While he may have had the upbringing and talent to go far in the wrestling business, his road to the WWF was no easy one. Although he was born in the Big Apple, he didn't stay there for very long. The main part of his childhood was spent in Winnipeg, Manitoba, where his dad was born and raised. "My dad was from Winnipeg and he used to play for the Rangers. I was born during the season [in New York] and in the off-season we lived in Winnipeg," explained Jericho.

Many people wonder why Jericho, born Chris Irvine, who grew up in Canada and is the son of a former pro player, decided to strap on a pair of wrestling boots as opposed to lacing up a pair of ice skates. But from early on, he knew where his future lay.

"I've played hockey all my life, [but] I wasn't good enough to play professional because I quit hockey when I was 16 to start training for wrestling," he said. "I decided I wanted to do that more. I still play hockey to this day."

As a matter of fact, the WWF grappler took part in a celebrity hockey event called Super Skate this past winter in Madison Square Garden, the site not only of his dad's former home rink, but also his current stomping ground when the federation is in New York. "Y2J" would not only score a pretty goal on this night, but in typical wrestling (or should I say Irvine fashion) he started a bench-clearing brawl. It just goes to show you that, skates and all, you can take a wrestler out of the ring, but you can't take the ring out of a wrestler. Just like that infamous night in Chicago, Jericho likes to leave his mark wherever he goes.

And believe me, this young grappler has been all over the

wrestling circuit and has left his mark worldwide. The standout athlete and student watched AWA wrestling from the age of ten; his dad would take him to see it at the Winnipeg Arena each month. The AWA then was replaced by the WWF in his area, but that didn't stop him from going to the arena for his wrestling fix. A few years later, when in high school, he caught Stampede wrestling and even managed to see some Ultimate Wrestling Federation during his spare time. During his teen years, he honed his athletic skills not only on the rinks playing hockey, but also in another water-based sport—polo.

Irvine said, "The only other sport I played in high school [besides hockey] was water polo because my friend and I wanted to try out for some kind of sport and all my school had was basketball, volleyball and water polo. I was too short to play basketball and I didn't like volleyball, so we tried water polo. It's actually one of the hardest sports I've ever played."

But even as he played and excelled in both of these sports, his mind still remained on making it into the pro rings. Irvine was glued to his seat watching Hulk Hogan and Owen Hart and many other wrestling greats ply their trade. As a matter of fact, he didn't care if he was watching AWA, WWF, Stampede or the old UWF, as long as it was pro wrestling. He was caught—hook, line and sinker!

"I always loved Hulk Hogan. I was the perfect fan," he explained. "I loved all the good guys and hated all the bad guys. I would do crazy cheers for all of them and boo the bad guys and get in their faces when they came into the ring."

But wrestling wasn't the only hobby for this Canadian teenager. He also loved music, especially heavy metal, and was into bands like Metallica, Twisted Sister, Iron Maiden and Quiet Riot.

The young Jericho was even able to convince his mom to buy him a bass guitar—even though he had no idea how to play it. After several long years of practicing, he became a natural and was ready to rock! He went through several different bands—Fatal Axadent, Destiny, Primitive Means and Mr. Filthy—before he found the right mix.

The mix for his band consisted of Jericho and two of his childhood buddies, K. S. Ashoff and Warren Rumpel, and they called themselves Scimitar. Irvine on stage then was just like the wrestler of today—he manned the mic and loved performing in front of crowds. Ashoff, who is one of his oldest friends, also liked to sing and play the guitar, while Rumpel played the drums.

Although Rumpel may not have been Irvine's first choice to man the skins, he was given the job for two reasons—he had a paper route and thus could afford to own a set, and he had a huge, unoccupied basement where the band could practice until five-thirty each night.

They practiced and polished their skills until they felt they were ready for the big time—their high school Battle of the Bands! The threesome envisioned rocking the teen nightclub, Flipside, like no other band before them. They saw Scimitar not only running away with the contest and sending their classmates into a frenzy, but also being offered a major record deal afterward.

Well, the band went on third that night, and boy, did they leave an impression! They were slated to play two songs, one cover and one original. They chose Megadeth's "Peace Sells" as the cover and their own "City Nights" as their original. When it was time to rock and the MC called for Scimitar to jam, they came running on stage. They plugged in their instruments—or did they?—and were ready to rumble. Their fans (friends) roared upon their entrance and the trio went right to work. They sounded great for about fifteen seconds, then the sound went dead and you could just about hear everyone breathing.

But a couple of moments later, the power was restored and Scimitar was back in business. They nailed their two songs and had fun doing it. Although they lost out in the next round and parted ways soon after, it was a most memorable experience for Jericho. He not only currently still performs from time to time, he also has a monthly column, "Metal Is Jericho," in hard rock's premier music magazine, *Metal Edge*.

But enough about the Ayatollah of Rock 'n' Roll-a's music background. Let's get back to his rockin' of opponents between the ropes. Upon graduating from college with a journalism degree, he decided to go all out after his dream of becoming a pro wrestler.

The first step he took was to pick up and move from Winnipeg to Calgary so he could enroll in the wrestling school known as The Dungeon, run by the famous Stu Hart in his basement. He trained there with several up-and-comers such as Chris Benoit, the late Brian Pillman and one of Hart's sons Bruce. They trained long and hard for three months, from June to September 1990. Irvine made his pro debut only one month later, on October 2, 1990.

Using the name "Chris Jericho," he worked the independent circuits in 1991 and 1992 and often teamed with Lance Storm in his indie travels. It wasn't long before he would get his first taste of a championship, as he would strap on the gold in January 1992 when he won the Canadian Middleweight belt.

From there he moved onto Bay Area Wrestling, which took place on the west coast in San Francisco in August. He stayed on the West Coast for three months until he once again packed his trunks and headed for the border. He now found himself working in Monterey, Mexico, where he formed a new identity, wrestling under the name "Corazon de Leon." The name, which means "lionheart," fit his style of wrestling because he not only wrestled with the heart and ferociousness of a lion, but he also adopted the high-flying quickness of the luche libre style in Mexico.

In January 1993, he left sunny Mexico and headed back north to Canada. This time he wanted to see if he had what it took to compete in a higher weight class. Not surprisingly, he was crowned the Canadian Heavyweight Champion. He took on Biff Wellington and made his countrymen proud, stripping the champ of his belt on January 29.

Three months later, the vagabond wrestler once again packed his belongings and headed back down south to Mexico. This time he debuted for the EMLL wrestling organization in Mexico City. Again Lionheart would strike gold, but this time he had to share in the glory, because a wrestler by the name of El Dandy and he won the WWA Tag-Team belt. They would defeat Texano and Silver King on July 21, 1993, for the right to be called champs.

Looking for a new challenge and challengers, the Lionheart decided to test his skills overseas in Hamburg, Germany for the CWA. He only stayed in Germany briefly before he returned to his old stomping ground, Mexico City, where he proceeded to stomp on any and all who wanted to challenge him. It didn't take him long to earn another golden strap—this time, he won the NWA Middleweight belt from Mano Negra on December 4, 1993. One month later, feeling homesick, he hopped another plane to Canada and took on Steve Rivers in Calgary for the Middleweight Canadian belt, which he of course won.

Having already wrestled in Canada, Mexico and Germany, Jericho again decided he wanted to try something new and boarded a plane to Japan, where he would make his debut for WAR on February 24, 1994.

When Jericho is asked about his travels and his work in different countries, he seems to prefer Japan the most. He likes the people, the country and the federations and their style of wrestling.

"Japan's a great place," he said. "It's my favorite place (in the world) to work."

In March 1994, he hooked up with the Smoky Mountain Wrestling (SMW) organization, which is located in Tennessee, and stayed with the federation for a year. While he grappled in SMW, he met up again with one of his former tag mates, Lance Storm, and they formed another partnership, calling themselves The Thrillseekers. This would prove to be a busy month for the young wrestler, as he would wrestle in three different countries. Not only did he step between the ropes in the United States in Tennessee, he also made his way to Mexico, where he won the Junior Heavyweight Tournament from Negro Casas in Mexico City; and to Japan, where he lost in the finals of the WAR International Junior Heavyweight Tournament to Gedo.

But this reign wouldn't last long for Gedo—Jericho defeated him three months later in Japan and was declared the International Junior Heavyweight Champion. Jericho would have to defend his title one month later on July 7, 1995. In an intense battle, he faced and beat Ultimo Dragon on this night in Japan and retained his title belt. Five months later, having earned all this gold and experience, Jericho decided to enter the prestigious wrestling tournament, the Super J Cup. Although he only advanced into the second round, he made an impressive showing in his loss to the Wild Pegasus, Chris Benoit.

His next stop would be Philadelphia, Pennsylvania, where he hooked on with Extreme Championship Wrestling and made his debut on February 2, 1996. From here on in he would split his time between the ECW and Japan, as he wrestled for championships almost each time out. Twenty-one days after his debut in Philly, he be teamed up with one of his former foes, Gedo, in Japan, where they won the WAR International Junior Heavy Tag Team belts. Three nights later the champs would have to defend their crown against Jushin Liger and Takaiwa, and they would do so in stunning fashion, as they worked the match like a well-oiled machine.

In June 1996, Jericho took part in the Antonio Inoki World Peace Festival in Los Angeles, where he would wrestle against Bam Bam Bigelow and Konnan. At the end of the month he captured his first ECW belt, the TV title, against Pitbull number two.

Lionheart was now on the verge of wrestling with the big boys. He was spotted by a WCW scout who offered him the chance to come and wrestle for them. He immediately signed on the dotted line. When asked if he was happy about coming to work for one of the Big Two as opposed to wrestling for the smaller indies, he had this to say: "Are you kidding? What idiot would say no to an exclusive contract with a group as huge as WCW? Here was my big chance, and I wasn't gonna blow it."

And he didn't. He made his debut with the federation on August 20, 1996, and never looked back. Twenty-six days later he was wrestling Chris Benoit on a WCW Pay-Per-View and four months later he would be given a new title as WCW Newcomer of the Year. Not bad for a former polo player, huh?

"I'm honored to be accepted by the WCW," he stated. "Many of its big name wrestlers were my favorites when I was growing up and now I'm in the ring wrestling with them. But more than that, I intend to give it my best, to make a name for myself and climb the ladder quickly but honestly. Wrestling is the greatest sport and I care about it in general and my reputation in particular. I'm going to always give it 110 percent and I hope the fans will be behind me."

While he always wanted to wrestle in one of the Big Two, the timing of his arrival in the WCW was a bad one for Jericho's career. He came onto the scene about the same time that a pack of super-star veterans arrived from the WWF. So although his skills were becoming polished in the ring, he was still unsatisfied, because his character wasn't going over well with the fans. The crowd's response to Jericho seemed to be lukewarm at best.

It wasn't until he reacted badly in the ring to an unexpected loss that he got a response from the crowd. Jericho got the people's attention when he began breaking things, pounding his fists, cursing and throwing a tantrum. He then proceeded to storm off the set of a Nitro taping. He would apologize in the following week, claiming that it would never ever happen again. That wasn't to be the case, however—he snapped in the same manner after another defeat.

The new approach allowed him to achieve what every wrestler works for—a response from the crowd. Although the boos at one time outweighed the cheers, Jericho didn't care. The fact that he was being noticed was all that mattered to him. He had his follow-ing, whom he dubbed "Jerichoholics," and he also had a following who would just love to get on him once he entered the arena.

Of this change, he noted, "I remember the old sports writer of years ago who said, 'In professional contact sports, nice guys always finish last.' Well, I learned that eventually, though it took me a while. I've been kicked around and abused by some of the big names of the WCW and I was getting a little tired of being abused. So, I changed my ways and I decided to create a different attitude. If that's how I want to wrestle, then I have that right."

As for the fans who were still in his corner, he had this to say: "I call them Jerichoholics because they are addicted to me—they worship, admire and respect me—so many of them would never turn on me 'cause I'm too important to them. But a lot of fans don't like me anymore. They boo me and carry these big insulting signs at the arenas, but it doesn't bother me. I'm making big bucks and climbing to the top and that's what's important."

Even though he would garner six different championship titles while working for the WCW, the politics in the federation were beginning to wear on him both as a performer and as a person. He felt his talent was being held down and that he wasn't being given a fair shot to be a prime-time player.

"Everywhere I'd ever worked I'd always been kind of like a 'main event' guy and one of the focal points and always involved," he explained. "In WCW I haven't been involved as much as I would like to be. I mean there's no secret about that. And there's a lot of guys here and a lot of depth, but I still think there's more of a spot for me than I've been given."

When he first came on the scene, Jericho was just happy to be in the same arena as the big boys, but after putting in his time, he no longer accepted just being in the same building. He now wanted a piece of the big boys in the ring!

"Just like WCW says—'Where the big boys play'—and that's who I want to fight with; not these little chumps with no size or strength. I like tough competition. I'm not afraid of it and I'm always eager to take on any and all challengers. That's why Chris Jericho has gone so far in wrestling 'cause I'm ready for anything."

Just when it looked like The Lionheart was going to get his wish to grapple with the big boys, Goldberg in particular, the federation soured on the idea. They started a minifeud between Goldberg and Jericho, which looked like it would eventually lead to a featured match, but the angle was scrapped.

"That was something where WCW gave me this stupid little angle and I made it into something good," Jericho explained. "But Goldberg hated it. He hated the whole angle." As to why Goldberg hated the angle, Jericho explained: "He said, 'I don't do comedy; I'm a real character.' I told him [that] comedy or not, this is what wrestling is about: getting heat and getting people interested in the match . . . I guess Goldberg really didn't understand the business then. Meanwhile, [Eric] Bischoff kept trying to end it with a two-minute squash match on Nitro, but I refused to do that. I told him that if we were going to have a match, it had to be on Pay-Per-View. I told him that people would pay to see it; I knew it would draw money."

But the WCW matchmakers and Goldberg didn't agree with the young wrestler, and the angle was never pursued again.

"That's when I realized WCW had a lot of problems," Jericho said. "Here was a money-making thing and they saw it, but they didn't acknowledge it. It was stupid and really soured me on the whole company."

Well, he tried to stay focused and continue progressing, but

Eric Bischoff (with the aid from several jealous veterans) couldn't come to terms with Jericho. When Jericho's contract expired, he became a free agent. It was now inevitable that the Lionheart would wind up in the World Wrestling Federation.

When he finally signed on to work in the WWF, Jericho felt like he was reborn—like a monkey had been taken off his professional back. He now felt he could fully use his talents to the max. All those years of training and traveling would finally pay off.

"I can honestly say—and I'm not a butt-kisser—but this is definitely the big time," he said in the November issue of *RAW* magazine. "This is the best company I've ever worked for besides maybe New Japan Pro Wrestling, which is very similar as far as organization and direction. I've been in the company for only a few weeks and there are already T-shirt designs on the board. It took me two and a half years to design and get my own T-shirt created in WCW. It's not supposed to be that way. This is a company and we're all here to do the same thing, which ends up making it a successful business for everybody. . . ."

He also saw a difference right away in the in-ring personalities in the WWF as compared to the WCW. "Very different. Here, everybody from top to bottom basically hangs out with everybody," he explained. "This is the wrestling business and I'm sure there are egos, but they are a lot smaller here. You know who the boss is and we know who to answer to when something goes wrong."

Well, so far the WWF's self-proclaimed new party host hasn't done anything wrong. Although his WWF debut went over big with the fans and federation, don't think he wasn't nervous that night in Chicago.

"I'm not going to lie and say I wasn't nervous, but I was nervous in a way that I knew it was my time to shine. This was it, my time had finally come and I deserved it," Jericho said. "Not because I'm some kind of extraordinary talent or anything, but because I've been working my butt off for nine years to get there and I was ready for it. It was a huge entrance and a huge amount of hype, but I knew I could live up to it and people wouldn't be disappointed. I don't think I've disappointed so far."

He's certainly right about that. From his debut onward, Jericho has not disappointed anyone, but has displayed toughness and agility in the ring, and has also been a master on the microphone. On any given occasion, this young grappler can either stir up trouble in the ring with his opponents or send the crowd into a frenzy with his mic magic. "The thing I like the most about the World Wrestling Federation is that every guy who goes through the curtain has a character the people know and a reason to be on television which people know about. So, it makes it much easier to get reactions," he said.

But you can't get the reactions if you don't have the talent, and Chris Jericho definitely has the talent. It only took the blond bruiser four months to win his first WWF title, which he did December 12, 1999, in Ft. Lauderdale, Florida, when he defeated Chyna for the Intercontinental strap.

Big things are in store for this small (by WWF standards) grappler as he is ready to carry the federation on his chiseled back. He came to the WWF with the intention not only of making a name for himself, but also of saving the federation from itself.

The rockin' wrestler has dreams of someday wearing the Heavyweight Championship belt. Jericho's dreams should someday become a reality, because he has the talent, smarts and personality to be a WWF champion—now all he needs is the chance and a willing opponent!

"All hail the Ayatollah of Rock 'n' Roll-a . . . as things will never, ev . . . , ev . . . , ever be the same again!"

Mankind, Dude Love and Cactus Jack

REAL NAME: Michael Francis Foley

HEIGHT: 6'2"

WEIGHT: 297 lbs.

BIRTHPLACE: Long Island, New York

FINISHING MOVE: The Mandible Claw

FAVORITE QUOTE: "Have a nice day!"

THE saying, "Never judge a book by its cover," definitely applies to the wrestler known as Mankind. At first glance, you would never expect this grappler to be able to *Man*handle opponents way bigger than him in the ring and you would also never expect his favorite saying to be "Have a nice day!" But the masked wrestler is full of surprises.

One of the biggest surprises he pulled off this year did not come in the ring. Mankind, a.k.a. Mick Foley, penned his autobiography, *Have a Nice Day! A Tale of Blood and Sweatsocks* this past summer, and the book was on the bestseller list for several weeks. Who would have ever thought that a wrestler's autobiography would interest people, let alone be a bestseller! People underestimated the power that Foley's sock-clothed hand possesses. This wrestler proved that he doesn't always need a chair to knock people off their feet. The pen works just as well.

But Foley is used to overcoming obstacles. Just like he was underestimated in his writing skills, he was also misjudged for his wrestling talents. But those who belittled what he could do between the ropes would pay somewhere down the line. Either federation officials would pay by not cashing in on the success of this wrestling phenom, or opponents would pay by receiving serious blows to the noggin—courtesy of Mankind.

Speaking of cranial blows, Foley has had more than his share during his fifteen-year pro wrestling career. He has compiled quite an impressive injury list, and it's a wonder he has survived to talk about some of his wounds. During his rise to the top of the wrestling world, he suffered bumps and bruises of all shapes and sizes. Some were more serious than others, but through them all, one thing was for certain: No matter how severe the injury, Foley would always try to continue. As a matter of fact, there were even instances when he was about to be carried out of the ring on a stretcher, yet he still managed to make his way back between the ropes to finish off his match and foe.

It seems that Foley has injured each body part at least once. He has suffered six concussions, a broken jaw, a broken nose (twice), a broken cheekbone, a broken right wrist, a broken left thumb, lost four front teeth, swallowed four teeth, had two-thirds of his left ear ripped off, had a torn abdomen, a broken toe, had a separated right shoulder, fractured his left shoulder, dislocated his left shoulder, suffered second-degree burns, had bone chips in his right elbow, had broke ribs on five separate occasions and has totaled over 325 stitches during his glorious career. (See page 104 for a blow-by-blow list of his injuries.)

Despite having a history of physical and probably some mental damage, Foley is doing exactly what he dreamed of doing ever since he was a child. Born on June 7, 1965, on Long Island, New York, Foley was brought up in a sports-filled household. His dad, a high school athletic director on Long Island, loved sports and passed this passion on to his son. The two would go to Yankee games together and watch wrestling on the tube. Their love and interest for wrestling even went beyond television proportions, as both would also partake in a fantasy wrestling league at one time.

A young Foley would wrestle in his backyard with his friends and they would imitate their favorite federation stars in the comfort of their own homes. They would also sometimes break out the movie camera and film their matches and later replay and admire what they had accomplished on their lawns and in their basements. Foley was by far the most daring of his friends. As a matter of fact, years later when he turned pro, one of these tapes found its way to the WWF offices and they used the footage on one of their cablecasts.

Already using one of his future ring names, Dude Love, on the backyard battlegrounds, Foley was caught in action on tape leaping off the roof of one of his friend's houses—which was two stories high—and had only a pile of old mattresses awaiting him down below to help break the fall. It goes without saying that the Ward

Melville High School student's high-flying antics were as popular back then as they are today.

In 1985, a visit by Tommy Dee to his former high school campus played a major role in helping decide his future. His dad called him in March of that year while he was attending Cortland State University in upstate New York, to let him know that wrestling was not only coming to their hometown, but more importantly to his alma mater's gym. Still the athletic director at Melville, Foley's dad was able to convince Tommy Dee, the wrestling promoter for that night's event, to talk to his son Mickey about the pro wrestling industry.

At first Dee didn't give Foley any encouragement about pursuing a career in the wrestling business. The only things he seemed interested in getting from the young fan were some grappling videos that his wrestlers could watch in the green room before they went on. Being the big fan that he was, Foley was able to supply Dee with some pro shows that he had taped at a previous time. When he went home to get the videos, he came up with a great idea—he would slip one of his teenage wrestling tapes in there to show them that he was serious about becoming one of them.

Well, a strange thing happened on the way back to the gym that night. He got there well before the show, and some current Melville students recognized Foley and stopped him. They wanted to know if any of the tapes he was carrying were of his famous backyard wrestling. Always taught by his mom to tell the truth, he told the students that one of them was. They begged him to play it for them and at first he refused, as he had to get the tapes to Dee for the pro wrestlers. But, when the students kept insisting, he gave in. After all, they were his fans and he didn't want to disappoint them.

He went into a room with a TV and VCR set up and played his infamous wrestling video. What started out as a handful of students ended up as a mob scene. The group was getting more and more excited and louder as they watched the teenage Foley work over his opponents. Amidst the dozens of students watching the video was Dee, who was impressed by what he saw on the tape, and more importantly by the reaction of the viewers. Foley was a drawing card well before his time!

After witnessing this, Dee had a change of heart and offered Foley a job as part of his ring crew; Foley would help set up the rings at Dee's events. Even though it wasn't going to be a glamorous job, he accepted the offer because it meant he was going to be around pro wrestling—better yet, he was going to be around pro wrestlers! Dee also made him another small promise—which would be his biggest break of all. He would have some pro wrestlers show him the ropes on occasion when the ring was completely set up and his job was done. This was great incentive for Foley to build that ring as quickly as he possibly could.

During the course of his blue-collar work, Foley met up with wrestling greats like Larry Zbysko, Sgt. Slaughter, Bob Backlund, Dominic DeNucci and Rick Martel. But of all these wrestlers, one guy in particular was responsible for helping Foley become a pro. That person was DeNucci. The pro wrestler would take a liking to the young crew member and would teach him some tricks of the trade before his matches.

When he saw that Foley was truly serious about wanting to become a wrestler, he offered him the opportunity to train at his gym in Pittsburgh on the weekends. But there was a catch—the youngster had to stay enrolled in college. He stressed to Foley how important it was for him to get an education, and he also warned the Long Island native how hard it was to make a living on the mat.

Willing to abide by DeNucci's rules, Foley was set to travel four hundred miles each weekend to learn how to wrestle, but he only had one problem. He couldn't afford to pay Dominic the $100 per session to learn to grapple. But being the great guy that he was, DeNucci agreed to let his student by on just $25 per day. Even though this was still a little steep for a college boy to pay, he still wanted to give it a try.

He survived on peanut butter and slept in the backseat of his car each Friday night for a good portion of two years, but it would all be worth it in the end. Believe it or not, attending DeNucci's training sessions also forced him to become more disciplined in his life. As a result, his college grades improved dramatically. In his senior year, the radio and TV production major would receive the Anne Allen Award for being the most outstanding student in his major.

Foley's parents were very proud of this accomplishment, as they never would've expected such a thing to happen to their son who only a few years earlier they had caught cutting class to go to a wrestling match at Madison Square Garden. What they didn't realize was that their son didn't cut college to go to just any old match. His idol, Jimmy "SuperFly" Snuka, was going to be wrestling that night in a cage match and Foley just couldn't miss seeing him perform in person his flying bodyslam off the top of the cage.

What Foley didn't know was that while he was watching Snuka from the third row at the Garden, his parents were watching *him* watch Snuka at home on their TV. The young Foley would learn two things from this experience. The first was Snuka's impressive, high-flying maneuver, and the second was to never, ever again buy a seat in the third row of a wrestling event that's airing on TV when you're cutting school.

But in order to become like Snuka, Foley knew he had to work hard both in the ring and on his studies. He also had to work overtime in keeping his wrestling training a secret from his friends. He told them that he had a girlfriend who lived far away and that he went to visit her on weekends. But after a while they were onto him because they not only saw sleeping bags and empty peanut butter jars in his backseat, they knew that their friend was in no way a ladies' man. "Could he be wrestling?" they wondered.

During his training at DeNucci's school, Foley would not only learn the ins and outs of the pro wrestling business and pick up some impressive moves, he would also learn the art of survival on the road through his car-sleeping experience. He would also train with several other wrestlers who would become important figures in his life and career down the road, including Troy Martin, later known as Shane Douglas; and Brian Hildebrand, later known as Marc Curtis.

On June 24, 1986, he would make his debut in the ring in Clarksburg, West Virginia, after being tutored by DeNucci for only two months. Although he was pretty nervous about making his debut, he wasn't about to stress out too much because he was originally scheduled to take part in a Battle Royal. No one would notice if he made a mistake, since several different wrestlers are in the ring at the same time. But the plans had changed. DeNucci approached him in the locker room and informed him that he wanted Foley to square off against another one of his students, Kurt Kaufman, in the night's second match.

Kaufman, who had previously wrestled professionally for a couple of indie circuits, tried to calm Foley down before the match. It did the rookie no good. He was a total wreck both before and during the match. Screwing up several maneuvers, Cactus Jack (as he was known that night) collided several times with Kaufman during their contest. Even though he lost his first match, something good did come out of the night—he met Brian Hildebrand. Hildebrand would not only join DeNucci's stable of wrestlers, he would also become Foley's first-ever wrestling manager.

The summer of 1986 would be a memorable one for Foley. Several of his wrestling classmates and he would be approached by DeNucci to work as jobbers (somebody who gets paid to be thrown around in the ring) for Vince McMahon's World Wrestling Federation. He immediately accepted the WWF offer.

His first stop would be Providence, Rhode Island, where he paired with Les Thornton in a tag match against the British Bulldogs, Davey Boy Smith and Dynamite Kid. He was even more nervous on this night than he had been in Clarksburg, because he was now going to be wrestling on the same card as some of the greats he'd watched when he was young. But this night would not be a disaster. Although he again lost the match and took some bumps and bruises, he felt he held his own, unlike in West Virginia. He had wrestled a pro match and lived to tell about it.

His next stop before going back to school was Hartford, Connecticut. This was a special event for him because not only would he be in the ring with the pros again; this time his parents would be there to cheer him on and tell him how proud they were of him. He proved to his parents that what he was doing was for real, and he would also lose two teeth that night in his match with Terry Gibbs against the Killer Bees in the sold-out Civic Center.

Foley worked a couple of more months as a jobber for the WWF. After that, when asked again to fight by DeNucci and the federation, he declined because he didn't want to be known as just a fill-in. He had gotten some great experience, but felt it was time to move on. He seriously wanted to make it in the pros and he knew that if he stayed on as a jobber, he might never get a chance to be a main-eventer.

Foley's choice wound up paying off—he got a call from Bill Watts one month after declining the WWF invite, asking him to work for the Universal Wrestling Federation (UWF). He would now juggle his full-time college schedule with the UWF schedule, leaving very little time to see his family or have a social life. But at the time, all that didn't matter to him, as he was not only doing well in his studies, but he was also making a name for himself on the grappling circuit.

In March 1987, the UWF was sold to Jim Crockett, owner of the National Wrestling Alliance organization. Foley, who felt that he and his fellow UWF wrestlers were going to be buried behind the NWA grapplers, was concerned. But Crockett actually had big plans for Foley. He wanted his Cactus Jack character to be a full-time main-eventer when he graduated in two months. The only thing that would change Crockett's mind about keeping Foley on as a full-time wrestler was if he royally messed up his debut match. That wasn't even an issue, since Cactus Jack had already wrestled in the big time with the WWF. This match was going to be a piece of cake for Foley. Or at least, it *should* have been.

His debut for his new boss took place in Johnstown, Pennsylvania, against Sam Houston, the half brother of Jake "The Snake"

Roberts. Everything was going well that night in the match until—Houston, we have a problem!—Cactus Jack literally fell flat on his face and his whole brief wrestling career flashed before his eyes.

He had overreacted to a Houston elbow, which never even came close to hitting him, and embarrassed himself and his opponent in front of two thousand people. Needless to say, he was not invited back after that blunder. But DeNucci, who was also present that night, would once again come to his rescue.

DeNucci had an out-of-the-country gig planned for two weeks after Foley graduated college. He asked the young grappler if he wanted to come along and wrestle at the event. Foley was more than happy to accept DeNucci's offer, and was thrilled to learn that he would get paid $3,000 for the two-week event in Burkina Faso, a small third-world country in West Africa. The paycheck, which was personally guaranteed by the country's president who was sponsoring the event, was a lot of money at the time for an inexperienced wrestler, so he wasn't going to complain—at least, not yet!

Foley's bad luck streak would continue; not only did he have a miserable time in Africa, he also never received his $3,000 payment from the West African government. He came back to the United States to a newspaper headline that read, GOVERNMENT OVER-THROWN, PRESIDENT ASSASSINATED.

Several weeks later, still desperate to stay in the wrestling biz, he tried his luck again with Africa, and this time it worked out for him. He spent six weeks on foreign soil plying his trade. He returned home from this tour $480 richer, and worked several different blue-collar jobs—as a landscaper, bartender and bouncer—until another wrestling break came his way.

Sadly, Foley was now at a point in his life where he could no longer afford to drive out to Pittsburgh on the weekends and train with DeNucci. When he informed his Italian grappling mentor of his dilemma, DeNucci hooked him up with a local Big Apple booker, Mark Tendler.

After wrestling for Tendler for some time, his next offer would come from Randy Hales, who ran the Championship Wrestling Association (CWA) down in Memphis, Tennesse. Foley ended up loving working for the CWA about as much as he had loved his travels to Africa. The only bright side to wrestling for the CWA was that he was getting much better money than he had in Africa. Foley was tired of working for a federation that didn't appreciate his talents.

One of the few good things that came out of the CWA was that he strapped on his first championship gold in his young career. Even though his first title had to be shared—it was a tag-team championship—he didn't mind as long as he had his own belt to wear! Foley and his ring-partner Gary Young had earned the right to be the number one duo in the independent promotion.

But he jumped at his first chance to leave the CWA, and found himself wrestling for the World Class Championship Wrestling organization in Texas. Here Foley would have a good time and a good run in the ring. He would also change his stage name from Cactus Jack to Cactus Jack Manson. Well, actually, *he* didn't change his ring name—one of his fellow grapplers did. The new moniker was given to him by Eric Embry, and it was in tribute to one of Foley's fans, who just happened to be stalking her favorite wrestler. Yes, that's right, Cactus Jack had a stalker! That was the first sign of his celebrity status.

After Texas, Foley wrestled for a small-town federation in Mont-gomery, Alabama. It was during this time that he got a phone call that would bring him back to wrestle for one of the Big Two.

Foley would get a phone call from Chris Adams, who was now working for the WCW under the name of Shane Douglas. Douglas would invite him to come to Atlanta to see one of his tapings for the WCW, hoping that his friend could catch a break from someone in the federation.

Well, Foley not only got noticed by Ric Flair, he was also told to come back in two weeks for what he thought was going to be a tryout. It turned out that the callback was not for a tryout, but was in fact an actual match, where he was paired up with R. Fargo against the mean and talented Steiner Brothers, Rick and Scott.

The talented Foley so impressed Flair during the match that he was immediately hired full time. Finally, he was now going to earn a real wrestler's paycheck, as opposed to the paperboy wages he'd been earning with the independent leagues.

He wouldn't wrestle his first singles' match until several weeks later. But when he did, he didn't disappoint. He would debut in his first one-on-one contest against up-and-coming Flyin' Brian Pill-man. And although he lost the match against Pillman, he would gain the attention of the fans and his fellow WCWers.

His action-packed debut bout lasted almost ten minutes. When he refused to leave the ringside area after he lost to Flyin' Brian, he was manhandled and roughed up for being a sore loser by Sting, a federation favorite. These postmatch antics by Foley and Sting had the crowd cheering and begging for more.

He stayed in the federation until June 1990 and then he moved on, as the WCW no longer appreciated his style of wrestling. He once again worked the independent circuit, which included some work for Extreme Championship Wrestling in Philadelphia. In 1991 Foley met the woman of his dreams, Colette Christie, in Long Island when Foley was working for an independent New York wrestling federation run by his first boss Tommy Dee. They were married a year later.

Along the way Foley wrestled future stars such as Sid Vicious, Ken Patera and Steve Williams. He also went overseas in 1991 to Japan, where he worked for All-Japan Wrestling for a while. When he returned home, he once again signed on to work for the WCW, "where the big boys play," as Cactus Jack. This time around he not only proved that he belonged with the big boys; he would become a father twice over. Colette gave birth to their son Dewey in February 1992 and one year later their beautiful daughter Noelle was born. Things were finally looking up for the young grappler as he beat wrestlers like Van Hammer and Paul Orndorff and eventually wound up feuding with the then–WCW champ Vader.

The two stars had all-out wars in the ring that set the fans and TV audience on their ears. Speaking of ears, Jack lost one of his lobes in a brawl with Vader in a March 1994 event in Germany. He got his head stuck between the top and middle ropes during the contest and when he tried to free himself the ropes ripped part of his left ear off. Being the trooper that he was, Cactus Jack continued to wrestle for another two minutes before he lost the match (and three-fourths of his ear) by pinfall to Vader.

This chunk of lost skin would also eventually make him lose his job with the WCW. He sued the federation for negligence, hoping he could get them to pay the $42,000 for the reconstructive surgery to his ear; but he lost on all accounts. First he lost a part of his ear, then he lost the match to Vader, then he lost the court case, and finally he lost his job! If it wasn't for bad luck, Foley would have no luck at all!

But success was just around the corner for Cactus Jack.

He landed back in Philadelphia for another stint with ECW. While there, he won the tag title with Mikey Whipwreck and battled Sandman in several memorable matches. He even had his Cactus Jack character turn heel during a 1995 ten-man tag match, where he unmercifully assaulted Tommy Dreamer. But he was soon in negotiations with the WWF to again join their outfit. His final ECW match would come a year later in March 1996 against Mikey Whipwreck in the ECW Arena in Philly. He was given a good send-off by his Pennsylvania fans, but he couldn't afford to look back as greener pastures awaited him in Stamford, Connecticut—the home base of the WWF.

The WWF signed him on for a second tour of duty, but this time they didn't want him as a jobber; they wanted him as a full-timer. But there was just one catch. Vince McMahon and company didn't want him as Cactus Jack, either. They wanted him to become this new masked character who they were originally going to call Manson the Mutilator. After some brainstorming, however, Vince and Foley settled on Mankind.

Well, Foley was none too happy at the time that Vince McMahon was basically telling Jack to hit the road, but years later he would be grateful, as his new character would go over like no other in wrestling. His Hannibal Lecter–like character would become one of the WWF's most popular personalities, and the fans fell in love with this character's crazy and high-flying moves.His popularity not only shot him up the ladder in the wrestling ratings, it also added a lot of zeros to his WWF paycheck. At the height of his popularity, his merchandise was second only to that of "Stone Cold" Steve Austin in total sales.

Mankind entered the WWF's squared circle in March 1996 and was matched up against Aldo Montoya, defeating him via his new finishing maneuver—the Mandible Claw! After several other feet-wetting matches, Mankind was off to feud with one the league's biggest personalities, The Undertaker.

The two would do battle like no other duo in federation history, their wars spanning well over two years. One of the highlight matches occurred at that year's King of the Ring tournament, which lasted over twenty minutes and saw Mankind with his arm raised in victory over the dark warrior.

Another unforgettable contest also occurred during Foley's freshman year in the WWF, when he again battled the 'Taker at the 1996 SummerSlam in a boiler room brawl. Mankind would not only steal another victory from his scary foe, but he would also walk off with the Undertaker's manager, Paul Bearer.

But the most memorable feud between the two personalities, Hell in the Cell II, was not only one of the best matches of the nineties, but it more importantly is remembered as one of the all-time best matches in the history of the sport.

In the 1998 King of the Ring tourney in Pittsburgh, the two squared off against one another in the Cell battle and all hell did break loose. Not only did each wrestler throw everything they had at one another, they climbed to the top of the sixteen-foot high cage and battled up there—not once, but twice! The match was a showcase for awesome moves, including the Undertaker flinging his opponent off the top of the Cell down through the announcer's table on the Civic

Arena's floor. Mankind would be scraped off the floor onto a stretcher, only to return moments later to again battle with the 'Taker.

The action picked up right where it left off and before you knew it, Mankind was pouring six thousand tacks onto the ring floor. Unfortunately for him, he would be the one to be at*tack*ed in the end, as The Undertaker would slam him to the mat and his body would receive the piercings of the little steel pins. But to his credit, Mankind declined the second stretcher and walked out of the arena on his own—well, almost—he was escorted by two of his fellow grapplers through the tunnel.

In the summer of 1997, Mankind would step aside for a new Foley character, Dude Love. The Dude, a tie-dyed shirt–wearing, chick-loving, hippie character, would make an "ass-whooping" appearance as a surprise tag partner of "Stone Cold" Steve Austin. The two would battle The British Bulldog and Owen Hart for the federation gold on July 14, 1997, and would come away victoriously as the new WWF tag-team champions. This would be the first of many tag-championship belts for him. Foley has totaled seven tag-title straps to date, having had the honor of working with Austin, Kane, The Rock and Al Snow in the process. He has won the most tag belts with Rocky Maivia, as the duo has captured three titles due to the almost unbeatable Rock and Sock connection.

In September 1997, the WWF would be blessed with a blast from the past, as Cactus Jack resurfaced. The mean-spirited character appeared on a Monday Night *RAW* that was being broadcasted from the world's most famous arena, Madison Square Garden. Cactus would send the sold-out New York crowd into a frenzy not only by coming back into the ring, but by also by kicking Triple H's ass!

Speaking of championships, Mankind would garner his first

World Heavyweight title in December 1998. He squared off against his former tag partner, The Rock, in Massachusetts, and beat his candy ass in front of a sold-out Worcester Centrum for the right to be called WWF champ. After beating his opponent for the crown, he took the microphone and dedicated the belt to his two adorable children, Dewey and Noelle. The proud father won the Heavyweight belt two more times in his hard-fought career, and he was also the first-ever crowned Hardcore champion in 1998 when the belt was first introduced to the WWF.

Cactus Jack would go out (supposedly) on February 27, 2000, the same way he came in—with a bang. He would wrestle Triple H, the WWF champ at the time, in a Hell in the Cell match. Not only was the belt on the line, but so was Jack's career. If he lost to Triple H, he would be forced to retire. If he won, he would gain his fourth heavyweight championship.

Although he would give Helmsley a pretty good beating, the fourth title strap just wasn't in the cards for Cactus Jack that night. He gave it all he had for his adoring fans, wrestling on top of the cell as promised. But in the end he wound up falling twenty feet through the top of the cage and onto the mat, where Triple H would eventually make his way down for the pin and win.

But to everyone's surprise, Foley would wrestle one final time. He was hand-picked by Linda McMahon to compete in a Fatal Four-Way Match with The Rock, Triple H and The Big Show at WrestleMania XVI in Anaheim, California, for the WWF Heavyweight Championship. Although he again failed in his attempt for a fourth world title, he didn't mind, because he was able to live out his dream of headlining a WrestleMania event.

What's in store for this hardcore wrestling legend is about as hard to predict as what character he will appear as next. But one thing is for sure about Foley—there will never be another like him in all of "mankind!"

MICK FOLEY'S BLOW-BY-BLOW CAREER INJURY LIST

4 SHOULDER INJURIES
Fractured left shoulder (December 1989, Long Island, New York)
Separated right shoulder (February 1990, Memphis, Tennessee)
Second-degree burns (January 1995, Honjo, Japan)
Dislocated left shoulder (June 1998, Pittsburgh, Pennsylvania)

7 FACIAL INJURIES
Broken jaw (August 1986, Providence, Rhode Island)
Lost two teeth (March 1986, Hartford, Connecticut)
Broken nose (March 1993, Atlanta, Georgia)
Two-thirds of his left ear ripped off (March 1993, Munich, Germany)
Broken nose (July 1993, Birmingham, England)
Broken cheekbone (May 1998, Milwaukee, Wisconsin)
Lost two teeth (June 1998, Pittsburgh, Pennsylvania)

1 STOMACH INJURY
Torn abdominal (September 1992, Atlanta, Georgia)

5 BROKEN RIBS
Broken ribs (March 1991, Sapporo, Japan)
Broken ribs (July 1991, Charleston, South Carolina)

Broken ribs (February 1992, Charlottesville, Virginia)

Broken ribs (December 1997, Durham, New Hampshire)

Broken ribs (June 1998, Pittsburgh, Pennsylvania)

4 HAND OR ARM INJURIES

Broken right wrist (May 1989, Fort Worth, Texas)

Fifty-four stitches to left arm (March 1995, Tokyo, Japan)

Second-degree burns to the right arm (August 1995, Yokohama, Japan)

Bone chips in right elbow (January 1996, Pittsburgh, Pennsylvania)

1 FOOT INJURY

Broken toe (July 1991, Baltimore, Maryland)

6 CONCUSSIONS

Concussion (July 1986, Quencas, Ecuador)

Concussion (August 1986, Providence, Rhode Island)

Concussion (October 1991, Lakeland, Florida)

Concussion (March 1993, Atlanta, Georgia)

Concussion (May 1994, Chicago, Illinois)

Concussion (June 1998, Pittsburgh, Pennsylvania)

Kevin Nash

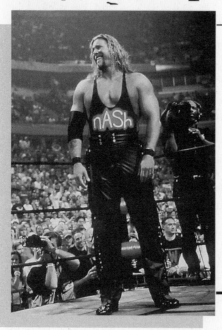

REAL NAME: Kevin Nash

HEIGHT: 7'0"

WEIGHT: 356 lbs.

BIRTHPLACE: Detroit, Michigan

FINISHING MOVE: The Jackknife Powerbomb

FAVORITE QUOTE: "nWo is just toooo sweeeet!!"

WHEN you talk about wrestling's "biggest" man on campus you must be talking about Kevin Nash. Even though he took a strange road to the bigs—he was discovered by some other pro wrestlers one night at a nightclub where he was working —it doesn't matter, as long as he got to the BIG time.

No one can deny that this seven-foot-tall, 356-pound wrestler not only has the size, strength, charisma and moves to be one of wrestling's biggest stars. But what many have questioned over the years has been the identity of his character. Who exactly is this guy and what direction does he want his career to go? Is he a bodyguard? Is he a babyfaced champion? Is he a heel? Is he the leader of one of the baddest wrestling gangs around? Is he one-half of one of wrestling's meanest duos? Who will show up . . . the good guy or the bad guy? Can he carry a federation for a long period of time?

These are just some of the many questions that arise whenever Nash enters the ring.

The easiest way to find out some of these answers is just to take a look back on Nash's background. Born Kevin Nash on July 9, 1959, in Detroit, the Michigan native was always into sports and literally stood a head taller than his friends, classmates and teammates, as he was already six feet tall at the age of fifteen. From an even earlier age, the talented athlete was pushed in a basketball direction, the efforts of which would pay off in the end for the young hoopster, as he jammed his way to an athletic scholarship with the University of Tennessee.

While at Tennessee, Nash once guided the Volunteers to the NCAA tournament, where his squad would make it all the way to the Sweet-Sixteen. His play was so impressive in college that at one time he ranked second among scouts only to Magic Johnson in NBA potential for players from the Michigan area. Upon graduation, he took his game to the next level and went pro. He packed his bags and played roundball in Germany for four years until a serious knee injury caused him to retire and come back home to the States in 1990.

Unable to play ball anymore, Nash had to rethink his career options. While pondering his future, he had to pay the bills somehow, so he worked in a nightclub in Michigan as a doorman and a bouncer. Little did the former ballplayer know that one night doors would be opened for him, instead of the other way around, as the nightclub gig would be the key to his future.

The opportunity of a lifetime happened one night for Nash when several NWA wrestlers showed up at his club. Having been a big wrestling fan growing up, Nash went over and shot the breeze with some of them, and they immediately took a liking to him. Judging by his size and personality, they suggested he look into trying out for their promotion. Looking for a new challenge and having nothing to lose, Nash took them up on their offer, and the rest is history.

Regarding the possibility at the time of becoming a pro wrestler, Nash felt he would be a natural not only because of his size and athleticism, but also because of his love for the sport.

"We always liked rasslin' around the house," he explained, "and I was always the winner. During my senior year in high school, I was bigger, meaner and stronger than they were. Heck, sometimes I beat [up] two guys at once. I was never afraid of anyone. Not only did I stand head and shoulders above them, but I'm sure I intimidated them as well."

His debut in the NWA was a sign of things to come as he entered the ring not as a wrestler, but as a bodyguard for a woman wrestler, Nancy Sullivan, appropriately named Woman. Woman was one-half of an NWA tag team called Doom. Unfortunately for Nash, or fortunately, depending on how you want to look at it, the bodyguard role only lasted a couple of weeks, because Woman's team split up. Nash was left without a job until he appeared in the federation several months later as a character named Steele, who was one-half of a new tag team called The Master Blasters.

The Blasters modeled themselves after another successful wrestling duo at the time, The Road Warriors, and tried to capitalize by bringing the Warriors' style of wrestling to the NWA ring. But much to their dismay, The Master Blasters' gimmick didn't fly in the federation. As a matter of fact, when the NWA talent was bought out by billionaire Ted Turner and turned into the WCW, The Blasters duo was terminated after Nash's partner Blade [Al Green] blundered big time in missing a flying head butt.

The next time the public would see Nash on the mat would be as a ludicrous wrestler with silver glittered hair known as OZ. The character was created with the movie *Wizard of Oz* in mind; Nash was outfitted in an outlandish costume and was escorted to the ring each time by a munchkin known as the Wizard.

He competed as OZ until 1991, when he was defeated by Ron Simmons. The OZ character was permanently sent back to Kansas after that loss. In this year, the pro grappler turned in his silver hair and tried his hand at acting, appearing in the movie *Teenage Mutant Ninja Turtles: The Secret of the Ooze* as Super Shredder.

When he returned to the ring scene, he took a gamble on a new personality named Vinnie Vegas. Although Nash was again clothed in a crazy-colored outfit, he thought this character might stick since he was paired with veteran grappler Diamond Dallas Page, but just like his other ring personas, Vegas was also unlucky.

Not one to give up quickly, Nash wanted to give the World Wrestling Federation a try. If there was anyone in the business who could make him a star, it was Vince McMahon. The grappler with long, blond hair would start his career in the WWF just like he did in the NWA: He came onto the scene not as a wrestler, but as a bodyguard.

Even though he already had gone down the bodyguard road before, this time would be different. Nash, now introduced to wrestling fans as Diesel, would be escorting one of the federation's prized wrestlers—Shawn Michaels—to ringside each night, which gave Nash, a federation rookie, huge amounts of exposure to the wrestling audience. Another positive difference was the look of his new character. Instead of being clad in outrageous colors, he was clothed in a black leather outfit, which really made him a threatening presence at matside.

His WWF wrestling debut would come at the 1994 Royal Rumble. As the seventh rumbler to come through the ropes, Diesel immediately went to work on whoever was in front of him. He faced established grapplers like Owen Hart, Bart and Billy Gunn, Scott Steiner, Bob Backlund and Virgil, and not only held his own, but made a name for himself by beating each one of these veterans. He bowed out after twenty long, hard-fought minutes in between the ropes, but there was no need to hang his head. Diesel had arrived that night, and the rest of the wrestling world took notice.

Nineteen ninety-four was to be a big year for the WWF freshman, as he now was no longer just considered another grappler's bodyguard, he was a legitimate contender in the federation. Through the course of the year he would prove to his new coworkers that he was there for more than just competing and surviving—he was there to win.

Diesel took the WWF by storm. His first stop was the Intercontinental title, which he took from Razor Ramon (Scott Hall) on March 13 in a matchup in Rochester, New York. Five months later, he won another championship, only this time he had to share in the glory. He won the tag-team title alongside the wrestler he used to guard, Shawn Michaels, on August 28 in Indianapolis, Indiana. The third and final belt he would garner in 1994 was the most prestigious of all—the World Heavyweight title!

Diesel would cop this strap in stunning fashion. On November 26 before a sold-out crowd in Madison Square Garden in New York, he beat grappling great Bob Backlund in an unheard-of eight seconds! In winning this championship, he became the first WWF wrestler ever to win three different titles in the course of one year.

But not all was rosy in the land of pro wrestling for the young WWF giant. His winning the championship strap didn't sit too well with his tag-team partner Michaels, a fact that spelled trouble not only for their duo, but also for their friendship. Michaels was known as a selfish, "me first" kind of guy, so any success his partner had—let alone a championship title—wouldn't flush in the bowl of "The Heartbreak Kid."

Diesel should have known three months before that Michaels wasn't too pleased with his success, because Michaels had "helped" his partner lose the Intercontinental title on August 29 in Chicago, Illinois to Razor Ramon by interfering in the match. Michaels should have been elated at the time for his partner in crime, since they had just finished winning the tag belts the night before. But instead, it seemed that the full-of-himself grappler once again let jealousy get the better of him. This all but spelled the end for the tag tandem.

Diesel was saddened by the way Michaels acted toward his success, and he wished things could have remained the same between the two of them both as a tag team and also as friends, but Michaels couldn't get over the fact that his one-time bodyguard won the World Heavyweight title before he did.

"Michaels thinks a lot like me," said Diesel, now known as Big

Daddy Cool. "We both believe in winning; no matter what it takes. It's unfortunate that he had to get so jealous over my becoming the World champ. We made a good team. No one was gonna take the title from us because no one was big enough to do it."

So two of his belts went just as fast as they came (Diesel and Michaels had to forfeit the belts due to their breakup), but Diesel wasn't about to let the World Heavyweight Championship belt go that easily. He held onto the strap for almost a full year before he lost it on November 29, 1995, in Landover, Maryland, to a two-time champ, Bret Hart.

The year 1995 would prove to be an up-and-down one for Big Daddy Cool. He reconciled with his former friend and tag partner Michaels, after he came to the aid of "The Heartbreak Kid" in April. Shawn, who at the time was being escorted to the ring by Sycho Sid, was getting the piss beaten out of him one night by his new bodyguard because he had just informed Sid that his services were no longer needed. Big Daddy couldn't bear to watch his ex–tag mate get pummeled, so he stepped in and saved the day.

Michaels was ever so grateful to Cool at the time that he not only agreed to rejoin his partner as a tandem in the ring, he also let it be known that he was not going to pursue the Heavyweight Championship as long as his friend sat on the throne.

"My number-one goal has always been, and always will be, to be the World Wrestling Federation champion," Michaels said. "I will never relinquish that quest. But for now, as long as Diesel is the champion, I will postpone my pursuit of the WWF title."

These were big words from a little man, but they wouldn't hold true for long. Michaels and Diesel would have another chance at a championship, and actually did win the belts back. But they were taken away the next night, when they didn't beat the true reigning champions for the title. The previous night, they had defeated Davey Boy Smith and Yokozuna, but the title holders were Yokozuna and Owen Hart, so the duo had to give the straps back.

Speaking of back—Diesel now had to watch his as he quickly became public enemy number one in the federation. Everyone not only wanted his title in 1995, they wanted a chance to chop down the WWF's biggest man to size. Throughout that year and into 1996, he would have awesome battles with Sycho Sid, King Mabel, The Undertaker, Bret Hart and his back-stabbing ex-partner and friend Shawn Michaels.

Not only were the wrestlers on his back at the time, but Diesel also had Vince McMahon and the WWF executives after him, as they kept changing and playing around with his story lines. It didn't matter that he was putting on a great show in matches with agile foes like Hart and Michaels; the executives wanted him only to do what he was told.

The big guy vowed not to be a "corporate puppet" and he started interfering in other wrestlers' matches, especially those of Michaels and The Undertaker. As a matter of fact, he cost The Undertaker his title at the 1996 Royal Rumble. The upstairs bosses and The Undertaker would make him pay for that little incident, when they plotted revenge on Diesel during one of his own title matches.

In a title match one night against Bret "The Hitman" Hart, Diesel would be pulled below the ring by The Undertaker, who popped up on him from virtually out of nowhere (he actually came through a trapdoor that was cut out in the center of the mat). Of course, this set up a confrontation between Diesel and the WWF's dark grappler.

The Undertaker and Diesel would square off on May 19, 1996, in Madison Square Garden at WrestleMania, and Diesel would be beaten to a pulp on this night by his powerful foe. Later on, Diesel would come back out and face off against his favorite opponent, Shawn Michaels. This match, which Diesel would lose by a pin to Michaels, would be the final contest for the towering wrestler in the WWF. He would later inform his friends and the twenty thousand crazed Garden fans that he, along with his pal Scott Hall, were leaving for the WCW.

In front of the crowd, Nash hugged and cried with his buddies Hall, Michaels and Hunter Hearst Helmsley, who had all gathered around him in center stage, since he knew it was going to be the last time they were in the ring together.

Nash and Hall, who would now wrestle under their given names, went over to the WCW and almost immediately wrought havoc on their new federation. They formed a duo known as The Outsiders and claimed to be the ultimate grapplers on the WCW roster. They also recruited one of wrestling's all-time greats on their side—Hulk Hogan—and formed a trio known as the nWo. The Outsiders would also form another group known as the Wolfpac with Sean Waltman (Syxx).

The Outsiders duo won the WCW tag belts an amazing six times since they went over to the federation. The first time they garnered the belts was on October 27, 1996, from the Harlem Heat in Las Vegas, Nevada. Their most recent tag title came on December 13, 1999, in New Orleans, Louisiana.

The nWo angle went over really well and allowed Nash to get back at his former boss Vince McMahon. The gang angle had the fans' interest and not only made for great TV, it made for cable wars on Monday nights.

Nash was once again on top of the wrestling world with the fans, but this time was different, because he came back to a federation where he had once been a flop, and made a name for himself.

He would continue his nasty ways even when he wrestled as a single. He started a bitter feud with The Giant (Paul Wight) in 1997 that was supposed to come to a head at Starrcade, but Nash was a no-show for the event. Many rumors circulated as to why the gigantic star didn't show (one was that he had suffered a mild heart attack), but he claims that it was merely a case of him missing his plane.

The two "giants" would eventually face one another at Souled Out that year, when Nash powerbombed his oversized opponent right into the doctor's office when The Giant suffered an injury to his neck. Nash's finishing move was then banned by the federation. They cited it as too dangerous for him to keep using in the ring, and that someday someone could get permanently injured from the maneuver.

But being the rebel that he was, Nash kept on using it. The powerbomb would begin costing him tons of cash, as the WCW was "fining" him $50,000 every time he used it in the ring. But Nash didn't care; he had his fellow nWoer Hulk Hogan bankrolling him. When the fines didn't stop him, the WCW brought in some "law enforcement" and had Nash put behind bars.

The seven-foot giant wasn't only stirring things up on the mat, he was also being a royal pain in the butt outside the ring. WCW head honcho Eric Bischoff tried to send a message to Nash by firing one of his members (Sean Waltman), but that only made the wrestler more mad. He asked to get out of his contract, but was denied.

Nash got into a battle with "Hollywood" Hogan, the end result of which was the nWo splitting up into two factions: nWo red and nWo black. No one was going to push Nash around anymore. He was no longer the new kid on the block.

Speaking of new kids on the block, Nash snapped rookie phenom Bill Goldberg's 170–0 unbeaten streak on December 27, 1998, in Washington, D.C., in one of the high points of his career. The Wolfpac leader has also garnered three WCW Heavyweight Championship titles to his credit, making a grand total of twelve world titles in ten years.

Not bad for a former bouncer and doorman, huh? Now he's bouncing opponents from the ring and people are holding open doors for him. Now that's "just toooo sweeeet!"

The Rock

REAL NAME: **Dwayne Johnson**

HEIGHT: **6'5"**

WEIGHT: **275 lbs.**

BIRTHPLACE: **Hayward, California**

FINISHING MOVE: **The Rock Bottom/ People's Elbow**

FAVORITE QUOTE: **"Know your role!"**

CAN you smell what The Rock has cookin'? Well, nowadays, whatever recipe this young grappler fires up turns into a five-star gourmet meal. The $500 silk shirt–wearing warrior has not only evolved into one of wrestling's most popular personalities, he has also kicked some serious ass in the ring, as can be seen by his rapid ascent to triple-crown winner!

Forget the Honky Tonk Man. Rocky Maivia is the World Wrestling Federation's Elvis Presley. While he may not be the king of rock and roll, The Rock definitely can be considered the king of "know your role." He is constantly preaching this saying to his

Rockaholics, who have become way too numerous to count. He is a firm believer that anyone can become anything they want to be as long as they "know their role" and get an education.

"First and foremost, finish school," Maivia has said. "A lot of times I heard it growing up and it went in one ear and out the other. 'Finish school. Get your degree. Nobody can take it away from you.' When I was told this I was like, 'Yeah, yeah.' But it's the truth. Once you make the effort, the sky's the limit! In wrestling, it takes a lot of hard work and it's even harder to make it."

And make it he did. But his road to the top was anything but direct.

It's safe to say that wrestling is in The Rock's genes (or trunks, in his case) as he is a third-generation grappler whose father and grandfather both wrestled professionally. He was exposed to wrestling from an early age, sitting on his grandmother's lap and watching his grandfather, "High Chief" Peter Maivia, go to work for the World Wide Wrestling Federation.

Grandpa Maivia was not only a legend between the ropes; he was also known as one of the classiest and toughest guys of his generation. He gave respect and commanded it in return from his fellow grapplers, and when he didn't receive it, look out! Legend has it that he once threw one of his colleagues through a glass window for making fun of him while he was eating. Being the gentleman that he was, however, he went over and helped the guy up. The former Texas Heavyweight Champion and U.S. Tag Champion taught his grandson how to be truthful and loyal, yet stern in a business where honesty and faithfulness are almost nonexistent.

The "High Chief" wasn't the only family member who would have an impact on The Rock's future. His father, Rocky "Soulman"

Johnson, also left a lasting impression on the wrestling world. Johnson, who teamed up with High Chief a couple of times as a tag team, wound up marrying the older man's daughter Ata. Maivia didn't approve of the union at first because he didn't want his daughter involved with anyone from his profession, but eventually everything worked out for the best, especially when Ata and Rocky had a son.

Johnson, whose career ran from the sixties into the eighties, was a true groundbreaker in the sport. He was the first African American champion in Georgia and Texas, the first African American to win the WWF Intercontinental title and also one-half of the first all-black tag team in the WWF to win a championship title. He garnered the coveted title belts with his partner Tony Atlas in 1983. The legendary wrestler also won tag-team titles in Canada and in the National Wrestling Alliance. This pioneer wrestler not only taught his son how to be a champion and how to strive for perfection in his life, but more importantly, he taught The Rock how to wrestle.

Dwayne Johnson did travel many roads before he got to be The Rock. Growing up, he lived in thirteen states and even had the chance to experience living in New Zealand for some time due to the nature of his father's job. Although he loved to watch his father and grandfather wrestle, he was still unsure about whether or not he was going to follow in their wrestling bootsteps.

Tipping the scales at six-foot-four, 225 pounds by the tender age of fifteen, he was hard to miss among his high school classmates. As a matter of fact, this is how he would get his first real (or amateur, in this case) taste of what it was like to step between the ropes. One of his high school teachers, who also happened to be the wrestling coach, approached him about joining their school's squad.

He was hesitant at first, but ultimately figured he'd give it a try. He showed up to a practice one day and immediately the coach pitted him against the school's biggest and strongest wrestler. So in pure Rocklike fashion, the third-generation wrestler kicked his "roody pooh" ass! Although he left his classmates in the gymnasium impressed, The Rock himself was not. As a matter of fact, he found amateur wrestling to be "boring," so he quit the very next day.

Instead he turned his attention to another rough-and-tumble sport—football. He put his family's business on the back burner and set his sights (or eyebrow) on greener pastures. The tremendously gifted Dwayne, whose family resided in Bethlehem, Pennsylvania, during his teen years, tackled football with ease and almost immediately became an accomplished star on the high school level. The defensive tackle was not only voted an All-American, but more impressively he was named one of the top fifty high school football players in the entire country (eighth best in the state of Pennsylvania). Because of his talents and achievements on the gridiron, he was widely recruited by many top colleges who had Division I football programs. The ironic thing about his final choice was that he chose a school that didn't even attempt to recruit him.

When all the recruiting letters and phone calls were pouring in, the defensive tackle made up his mind that he wanted to attend a college in a warm climate. He began to focus on the state of Florida. As a matter of fact, he had even given the powers that be at Florida State University a verbal agreement that he would attend their school. But Dwayne was curious why the University of Miami wasn't calling to recruit him. So he decided to take the bull by the horns and call them himself.

After calling the school's athletic office he was put through to the football recruiting coordinator. Once he got the full Rock treatment, the recruiter was sold and agreed to send out a letter of intent. A few days later he received a phone call from the team's defensive line coach, and soon enough he was wearing the orange and white for the University of Miami. Dwayne had turned the tables on the coaches at the University of Miami and convinced them to recruit him instead of them trying to sell him on going to their university.

He claims that his decision to go to Miami and play football for the Hurricanes was an easy one, because out of all the schools that tried to recruit him for their college football program, the University of Miami was one of the few promising both a good education and a shot at a national championship. "He was interested because of the tradition that we had at Miami," said former Hurricanes coach Dennis Erickson. "He was also turned off by many of the colleges because of their crooked recruiting tactics."

After some tough times, Dwayne settled in and reaped the benefits of his athletic scholarship. He put his nose to the books and turf and wound up graduating not only with a degree in criminology, but also with two national championships (1989 and 1991). He aspired to work for the Secret Service after graduation, but once again his athletic ability took him in a different direction.

He would now try to take his football ability to another level (and country), as he was afforded a chance to play pro ball for the Calgary Stampeders of the Canadian Football League. What he thought was going to be an awesome experience turned out to be a horrible one. Instead of making the Stampeders, he was placed on the team's practice squad, which paid him $250 a week, or roughly $175 after taxes. He knew he couldn't live on this salary for long and that he had to start exploring other options.

"I made a decision to close up that chapter in my life and open up a new one," he explained in an interview that appeared in *Wrestling World* magazine.

There was always the family business, but Dwayne was no quitter. He was determined not only to become a star with the Stampeders, but also one day to play in the NFL. Well, his football dream turned into a nightmare when he received a call from his agent one day after practice telling him that Calgary was releasing him. Dwayne was crushed and immediately called home for his father to come pick him up.

On the ride back to the States, Dwayne told his dad that he wanted to try his luck with pro wrestling and that he wanted his dad to train him. Although his father was opposed to the idea and fought his son tooth and nail on the matter, "The Soulman" knew his boy was for real and if anyone was going to train him to be a wrestler, it was going to be him!

Through his dad's influence, The Rock got a tryout with the WWF. He impressed the powers that be enough that he wrestled his first match not long after the tryout. Surprisingly enough, The Rock won his first match, which was against the Brooklyn Brawler in Corpus Christi, Texas. Introduced simply to the crowd as Dwayne Johnson, the rookie was now 1–0. The federation booked him the next night to wrestle again. This time his foe would be Chris Candido. Candido would defeat Johnson in this match, evening his record at 1–1, but the freshman grappler didn't care—as he was just happy to be between the ropes.

Following his defeat, he received some bad news. Although he performed well above rookie standards, the talent coordinator didn't feel he was ready to compete in the big time on a nightly basis just yet. They offered Johnson the opportunity to work on his skills in Memphis, Tennessee, the home of the United States Wrestling Alliance, a training ground for up-and-coming WWF grapplers. Instead of being disappointed, the Hayward, California, native took his demotion in stride because he knew that, unlike his experience with the Stampeders, he was where he was supposed to be. He sensed that someday soon he'd be back in the ring, and, more importantly, he knew he was enjoying himself.

"I do what so many guys (athletes) wish they could do," he said. "That's why a lot of professional athletes are big fans of sports-entertainment [wrestling]. When a professional football player gets interviewed, they wish they can say what they feel! They wish they could say, 'We're going to go out there and kick the piss out of these guys and there's nothing they could do about it! If you smell what so and so's cookin'? But it's politically incorrect."

Now having to face a new challenge (and a very long drive to Memphis), he decided to spend his time thinking of a new ring name—something that was wrestling related, but also gave a hint of who he was. So Johnson came up with . . . Flex Kavana? OK, so it wasn't the best of names. He chose "Flex" because it was a muscle-related word and "Kavana" because of its Samoan origin. Not the best of choices, but then again, Johnson wasn't the best of wrestlers at the time, either.

He honed his skills in the minors for a good long six months, plus one more tryout match (against Owen Hart), before the federation decided to bring him up and keep him with the big boys full-time. He made his official WWF debut on November 16, 1996, at one of the federation's biggest events of the year, The Survivor Series, which took place in the Mecca of wrestling arenas—Madison Square Garden!

This night would be so different for Dwayne because not only would he dump the Flex Kavana ring name and wrestle in front of twenty thousand fans, he was now officially on the team roster. There was no turning back! He chose the name Rocky Maivia, which was first recommended to him by his mom when he entered the business, as a tribute to both his father and grandfather.

No one knew who he was when his name was first announced as a participant in the event on that infamous night in the Garden, but when all was said and done, each fan went home with the name Rocky Maivia ringing in their heads. The rookie would not only handle himself well in the ring, he would walk out of the arena on this cold November evening the champion of the Survivor Series!

Maivia had entered the World Wrestling Federation with a bang, debuting with a pin of a veteran (Goldust), an almost unheard-of feat for a freshman. Although the fans didn't like the fact that the rookie stole the glory that night, they seemed to realize that this newcomer was going to be around for a long time to come.

But just because Maivia was going to be around for a while, the fans didn't have to like him or cheer for him. As a matter of fact, they did just the opposite! Even though he was working the circuit regularly and racking up wins, the fans started to get on him more and more. The boos were becoming commonplace, and they were getting louder with every win!

This treatment not only baffled Rocky, it also made federation officials scratch their heads. Maivia was supposed to be a good guy—an ally of the fans. He had good looks, a babyface and smiled a lot, so what was the problem?

The federation ignored the fans' disapproval and kept Rocky on a winning pace. In 1997, the Survivor Series Champ added another title to his young career. Maivia took on the Intercontinental title holder Hunter Hearst Helmsley on February 13 of that year and to the crowd's surprise, he again came out victorious.

The boos took a turn for the worse in March 1997 in Chicago at WrestleMania XIII, when Maivia was supposed to defend his Intercontinental Title. The young grappler was so ecstatic to be a part of this huge wrestling event that he invited his family to come along and watch what he thought would be a night to remember. It did turn out to be a memorable event for Maivia and his family, but one they probably wish they didn't remember!

In defense of his title, the babyfaced grappler was scheduled to take on Sultan, a notorious heel of a wrestler. Maivia figured he would have the crowd on his side, since fans always cheer for the good guy over the heel. *Wrong!* The fans started booing Maivia the moment he entered the ring. By the time he had pinned Sultan and defended his belt, the jeers turned to chants of "Rocky Sucks! Rocky Sucks!"

The chant seemed to catch on. Everywhere Maivia wrestled, the crowd despised him. He dropped the Intercontinental Title and tore up his knee that spring, but not before the chants got louder and signs began popping up reading, DIE ROCKY, DIE!

Even though the signs and crowd's reaction to his wrestling began to weigh on him, Maivia would soon learn that all the negativity would eventually take his career on an upward swing. As he was rehabbing his injury, he was approached with the idea of changing his character from babyface to heel. He loved the idea immediately and couldn't wait to try out his new role on the fans!

In August 1997, Rocky came back on the scene, but he wasn't the same. He showed up unannounced during a match between Faarooq, the leader of The Nation of Domination, and a wrestler named Chainz. Chainz was kicking Faarooq's butt pretty soundly but he couldn't get a win because the ref had been knocked out cold earlier.

Taking advantage of the ref's unconsciousness, Maivia charged into the ring where the crowd thought he would help the good guy Chainz finish off the bad guy, but instead, in typical heel fashion, Maivia began to work over Chainz. He beat the good guy until he was dazed and confused. Then he proceeded to place Faarooq on top of Chainz so he could get the win once the ref came to. And that's exactly what happened. On that night, not only did Faarooq get the win, he also gained a member. Rocky Maivia was officially granted membership to N.O.D.

The crowd's reaction remained the same toward Maivia, but now he didn't care—*bad guys are supposed to get booed!*

Not only did Maivia's attitude change at this time, he also changed his ring name once again. He now simply wanted to be called "The Rock!" "Just take a look at me, I'm handsome, well-built, in better physical shape than many wrestlers," he explained. "I have everything going for me and that's why they call me The Rock! I am solid muscle, I am practically undefeated and the majority of the wrestling world is insanely jealous of me!" His cockiness was well off the Richter scale at this time in his young career. "Don't deny it. I can name any pro wrestler and you couldn't disagree with me that he would want to be in my shoes," he bragged.

The Rock was finally comfortable with his career. As a member of The Nation, the rookie wrestler would have some time to hone his skills away from the center of attention. In October 1997 he teamed up with a couple of his Nation buddies D'Lo Brown and Kama Mustafa (today's GodFather) and took on "The World's Most Dangerous Man" Ken Shamrock and the Legion of Doom.

This led to a series of nasty encounters between The Rock and Shamrock, but it was nothing The Rock couldn't handle. "Ken Shamrock has given me a run for my money," he explained at the time. "But like me he is in good shape and a tough man." That's about as close to a compliment you're going to get from this cocky grappler, so Shamrock should have been pleased to read that.

The two would meet again at that year's Survivor Series. The Rock was part of the N.O.D. squad that squared off against Shamrock, L.O.D. and Ahmed Johnson, but Shamrock would soon be old news. The Rock had something Stone Cold cookin' in his wrestlin' kitchen!

One evening during a RAW IS WAR event, "Stone Cold" Steve Austin was fighting off a bunch of N.O.D. members when The Rock literally stole the Texas Rattlesnake's Intercontinental Title belt. Actually, Austin was forced to relinquish the belt to The Rock per his boss Vince McMahon's demands. This was not only the start of another IC title reign for the cocky wrestler; more importantly, it was the start of one of wrestling's greatest rivalries—The Rock vs. Steve Austin!

At the Pay-Per-View event on December 7, 1997, The Rock and Austin would engage in one of the most memorable matches ever to take place in wrestling history. The Rock would be pinned by Austin and lose his IC belt and title . . . or would he? Austin knew he was only a couple of months away from superstardom, so on the following night at another RAW IS WAR event, Stone Cold handed the belt and title back to Maivia, claiming "he had bigger fish to fry!"

While some may have claimed that Austin humiliated The Rock and the IC belt by doing that, the fact of the matter was that Austin was ready to become World Champ and he just passed the torch to the next deserving contender. Being no roody pooh fool, he also didn't want to have to battle The Rock two nights in a row!

The tide was beginning to turn for the self-proclaimed "Most Electrifying Man in Sports Entertainment," as he was now not only getting the respect he always wanted and deserved from his peers, but was also starting to hear cheers instead of jeers from the fans. The sky was the limit for the twenty-seven-year-old phenom.

The next stop for The Rock would be San Jose, California, on January 18, where he would take part in The Royal Rumble. With the new year and a new attitude, the young wrestler was ready to take on any and all who wanted a piece of him. On this night he was scheduled to defend his IC title against a familiar foe and hometown favorite, Ken Shamrock.

Shamrock was talking up a storm in the arena that night before the bout, claiming that the only way The Rock was going to win was if he had help from his posse N.O.D. Well, The Rock not only promised that The Nation would stay out of the way, he also promised to kick Shamrock's roody pooh ass! And as promised, The Rock delivered on both accounts. He tortured The World's Most

Dangerous Jabroni for over twenty minutes in the ring before registering the win and successfully defending his title.

But The Rock wasn't finished for the night yet. He tossed himself into the Royal Rumble competition, which is a battle royal that has thirty wrestlers from the federation trying to be the last one standing in the ring. He was the fourth grappler to step through the ropes, and one by one he started laying the smack down on whoever was put before him. He was like a bull in a china store, wreaking havoc on the opposition.

This set the stage for the grand finale. The Rock saved some of his best stuff for last, as his opponent was none other than his nemesis "Stone Cold" Steve Austin. The two had a classic rumble in the ring, but on this night Austin was the better man. Although Austin came away with the win, The Rock gained something, too—invaluable experience in a main event.

A couple of months later, he would take part in his second WrestleMania, and this time he was ready for the big event. He had been here before, but this time he was squaring off against someone he was familiar with. Again he would battle Shamrock and dispose of the former Ultimate Fighting Champion. Things seemed to be getting easier and easier for the former gridiron player. He was a natural between the ropes!

With all of this sudden success and popularity, his status with The Nation began to change. Instead of being a background member of the gang, he began "to know his role" in the group, which started to cause rifts amongst The Nation. The most jealous Nationer was the leader of the pack, Faarooq.

Faarooq felt threatened by The Rock and sooner rather than later, he was ousted from his throne by Maivia. The Rock insulted

Faarooq on national TV one night by giving every N.O.D. member except him a Rolex watch. The Rock told the Nation leader he had "an extra special" gift for him. Something he would love more than a Rolex. He then preceded to give Faarooq a big color poster of himself. The picture, which was of The Rock holding his Intercontinental belt, so enraged Faarooq that he smacked a hole right through The Rock's face. The two then grappled in the ring until they were separated by the other members. This incident set up a match where the two members squared off against one another. The Rock would not only defend his IC title that night against Faarooq, he would also become the new and true leader of The Nation of Domination.

Shamrock would enter the picture again in June. As always, he badly wanted a piece of The Rock. The two tangled in Pittsburgh at the King of the Ring event. They would once again put on a great show, but this time the outcome would be different, as Shamrock finally got revenge on his rival and beat him. Shamrock was one step ahead of his opponent that night in Pennsylvania, and he managed to put an ankle-lock submission on The Rock. Although he couldn't add this title to his accomplishments on this night, that was OK because he was still the Intercontinental champ.

The IC champ would have a busy summer from there on out. He not only had to defend his title, he was also now the leader of The Nation and had to deal with gang warfare between N.O.D. and D-Generation X. This gang rivalry also spilled over into a personal grudge match between The Rock and DX's leader Hunter Hearst Helmsley. When the group feuds died down, The Rock–Triple H confrontations heated up. At SummerSlam 1998 in New York, HHH tried to combine insult and injury in his memorable match with The Rock. He showed up dressed like the People's champion, with Rocklike felt sideburns and a bad hairpiece. Apparently, Triple H "knew his role" on this day, as he went on to defeat The Rock and become the new Intercontinental Champion, ending The Rock's nine-month title run.

The grueling forty-five-minute ladder match was memorable in many ways. First, both heroes gave the fans their all between the ropes for almost an hour. Second, Triple H won the belt from The Rock in a unique way. The former DX member wound up gaining the belt at the match's end only because he had some assistance from his sidekick Chyna. His personal bodyguard laid the smack down between The Rock's legs as he was on his way up the ladder to grab the title belt for the win. But last, the most memorable thing that came out of this match was the crowd's reaction to The Rock. When the ladder match first began, Triple H had the crowd on his side as chants of "Rocky Sucks!" filled the arena. But in the end, echoes of "Rocky, Rocky, Rocky!" could be heard throughout Madison Square Garden.

The Rock's career was again looking bright—he now finally had the crowd on his side. Over the next few months he honed his mic skills, developed catchphrases that would be echoed through-out arenas worldwide, and put himself on the road to his first world championship.

At the Survivor Series in November 1998 in St. Louis, Missouri, The Rock would win his first world title under cloudy circum-stances. Although he would legitimately defeat three world-class wrestlers (Big Boss Man, Ken Shamrock and The Undertaker) on this night to get a shot at the finals and the championship belt, what transpired in the end was pretty shady.

His opponent in the final round was Mankind. At first it seemed as though this would work against The Rock, because Mankind was supposed to be Vince McMahon's hand-chosen new champ. So how could he win? How could he lay the smack down on Mankind without having any kind of outside interference? All in all, The Rock didn't need any outside interference—as a matter of fact, he didn't even have to pin his opponent to win, because as soon as he had Mankind in a sharpshooter hold, McMahon called for the bell.

As it turns out, The Rock, *not* Mankind, was in cahoots with The Boss! The Rock had fooled not only his foe, but also all the fans in the arena. He claimed the reason he did this was to teach the fans never to go against him. He said that he never forgot their "Rocky Sucks!" chants and that they could all now kiss his candy ass! The Rock had turned Corporate!

This was the beginning of yet another rivalry for The Rock. Mankind and he would engage in some unforgettable, if not violent, matches over the course of the next five months. Each wanted not only to defeat the other, but to also be the owner of the most precious federation title—Heavyweight Champion!

One month to the day of his first championship reign, The Rock lost his belt to the out-of-control wrestler Mankind in Worcester, Massachusetts. Not only was Maivia pissed and surprised at the outcome of the event, but Vince McMahon and his son Shane also weren't too thrilled. The two McMahons quickly went to work and scheduled an "I Quit," match where the loser of that event would have to do as the title states.

Never one to turn down a challenge, Mankind agreed to take part in the bout. The match took place in January 1999 at Royal Rumble in Anaheim, California, and was violent from start to finish. The two superstars engaged in a hard-core match where each man traded thunderous blow after thunderous blow. At one point in the match, The Rock took advantage of a worn-out Mankind and handcuffed his hands behind his back.

He then had the mask-wearing grappler kneel in the middle of the ring, where he proceeded to smash Mankind in the head with a chair ten times. The vicious wallops rendered the wrestler unconscious, but somehow he managed to utter the words "I quit," giving The Rock back his title. What the fans didn't know (neither did Mankind, because he was out cold!) was that Vince and Shane had struck again. The two McMahons had prerecorded Mankind saying "I quit," and had his voice played over the arena PA.

This title reign would be even shorter than the last one for The Rock. Two nights after stealing the belt from Mankind, he lost it again to his nemesis in a special WWF show that aired during halftime of the Super Bowl between the Denver Broncos and Atlanta Falcons.

Not wanting Mankind to wear their title belt, the McMahons again arranged for The Rock to have another title shot against Mankind less than a month later. On February 15, 1999, The Rock recaptured the title belt in yet another controversial title match. The ladder match, which took place in Birmingham, Alabama, was marred by outside interference by Team Corporate's newest member at the time, The Big Show (Paul Wight).

The multimillion-dollar wrestler had now achieved what no other wrestler had done in the history of WWF wrestling—he had become a three-time Heavyweight Champion at the young age of twenty-seven! Not bad for someone who only a few years earlier was bringing home $175 a week.

While he is one of the most popular grapplers today, The Rock has more to brag about than just his wrestling skills. He has appeared several times on the cover of many prominent publications, including *TV Guide*; guest-starred on several TV shows; and he even was involved with the Got Milk? ad campaign, where he posed for an ad that encouraged children to drink milk. He is also the author of a bestselling book *The Rock Says*.

The Rock, who resides in Florida and is happily married to his wife, Dany, loves kids and taking time out to sign autographs for his fans. He is a true champion in every sense of the word, and he gives back to the fans as much as he possibly can. He is a diamond in the rough, an athlete who tries to lead by example. The Rock not only walks the walk, he talks the talk, for he "knows his role" in today's society.

In his book, he writes, "There are a lot of demons in this business. I saw them firsthand when I was growing up and I see them now. If you're a successful, famous professional wrestler, the forbidden fruit is within easy reach. The groupies are there. The women are always there. And the availability is high. It's easy to go out and get laid. It's easy to go out and get drugs. It's easy to go out and drink. I don't condemn other guys for doing that. I will never, ever pass judgment. You live your life how you deem appropriate. . . .

"At this point in my career, going out to a busy club or bar is usually more trouble than it's worth," he explained. "If The Rock is hanging out in a bar at 2:00 A.M., he's practically asking to be hassled!"

Spoken like the people's champion that he truly is!

Sting

REAL NAME: Steve Borden

HEIGHT: 6'2"

WEIGHT: 252 lbs.

BIRTHPLACE: Venice Beach,
California

FINISHING MOVE: Scorpion Deathlock

PRO DEBUT: 1985

IN today's sports-entertainment industry, where personalities change their alliances and federations as often as they change their tights, Sting can be considered an exception to that rule.

He has remained loyal to World Championship Wrestling since joining their federation in 1987, with which he almost immediately became a star, and has basically played the role of good guy for his entire tenure in the Atlanta-based organization. Because of these choices, the Stinger has gathered a huge following during his fifteen-year pro career.

"I guess you could say I'm one of the few successful pro

wrestlers who's extremely happy with where I am," he explained. "The money is good, the exposure, the competition is excellent and I don't know what more I could want."

Born Steve Borden on March 20, 1959, in Venice Beach, California, the future wrestling star was always athletically active during his childhood. He was a member of both his high school and junior college wrestling and football teams, and also developed an interest in bodybuilding along the way.

"In school I was always one of the biggest and strongest guys on the team and therefore I went out for football and did quite well and that's when I seriously discovered weight training and bodybuilding," he said.

In fact, he not only discovered bodybuilding, but had serious thoughts about pursuing a professional career in the sport. He would regularly enter in competitions and had immediate success, placing second in his first-ever competition, the Mr. Los Angeles contest.

While Borden loved the challenge and weight training for competitions, he would soon learn that taking part in fitness contests was a totally different experience than wrestling or playing football. "I was pretty bulked and muscular, particularly considering it was my first bodybuilding contest and I was totally inexperienced," he explained. "But obviously I did pretty well. But I hadn't realized at the time the complete difference between training for a bodybuilding contest as opposed to say a football game or wrestling match.

"For example, the dieting is much more important for bodybuilding and I love to eat. I like steaks, salads, red meats, potatoes and most of them have quite a few calories. I need the bulk, weight and strength which I can turn into muscle for wrestling or other contact sports, but with bodybuilding, the diet is crucial," he said.

"The last two weeks of the bodybuilding contest I had to eat, in a whole day's meal, two pieces of fruit, a chicken breast, a salad with no dressing and raisins. Talk about starving!"

All of his training for that first competition had him not only looking great and standing on the podium with the runner-up trophy, but in the end it also made him raid his refrigerator like never before. "My body was shredded down, cut as they call it and I was totally ripped," he said. "You've never seen so many abdominals! Once I won that trophy, boy, the next day I was starved and I think I ate the whole kitchen. I think that day I had steak and eggs for breakfast; two sandwiches at lunch; then prime rib, salad and a baked potato for dessert [at dinner]. Oh yeah, and then there was the chocolate pie."

He would enter a few more competitions, but he knew bodybuilding wasn't for him. He wanted an athletic profession where he could combine his love for bodybuilding and competition without having to give up his love for good food. While waiting for his big break, Borden would work as a personal trainer in a local California gym.

In 1985 he would find exactly what he wanted. Hall of Fame wrestler Red Bastien would discover and train him, and would also ask him to join his PowerTeam USA organization.

"When wrestling came around," he said, "I knew then that was for me. I liked the big bucks, the travel opportunities, the great people, the stardom and the tough competition. I knew right then that was what I really wanted to devote all of my time to."

This PowerTeam organization was a federation that emphasized wrestling ability and great sculpted physiques, and Bastien knew a lot about both. He taught his students to give it their all and learn as much about the history of the sport and their opponents as possible.

And Borden took to his coach's philosophy pretty quickly. "That's kind of how I've always been with things I was interested in doing—I believe that old philosophy of do it right or don't do it at all. So while I was being trained for wrestling, I studied a lot about the sport in general, certain wrestlers in particular. My coach told me, and he was right when he said, 'You may eventually wind up in the same ring as these guys [so you should learn as much about them as possible.] You may [even] win a title from them.' And he sure was right.

"Even to this day I'm still studying and learning new things from various books, magazines, instructors, everything," he said. "You can never learn too much. I've always believed in experience, but more important than that I feel is education. And in the changing world of pro wrestling, you need to be up to date on the latest."

While he was a member of the PowerTeam, he met Jim Hellwig, later known to wrestling fans as The Ultimate Warrior. The two, who were inseparable at the time, then became known on the indie circuit as Flash (Borden) and Rock (Hellwig). After the PowerTeam disbanded, they formed an awesome duo known as the Blade Runners and wrestled in the Mid-Southern area, moving onto the Mid-South promotion.

The Mid-South would eventually turn into the UWF promotion, and Borden would eventually change his ring name from Flash to Sting. The duo didn't last very long on the circuit, because Rock continuously bumped heads with the league's officials. When Hellwig left for the World Class Promotion, Sting stayed in the UWF. Staying in the federation would pay off for him: he picked up his first two championship belts a short time after Hellwig's departure. The two belts he won were tag straps; he first teamed up with Eddie Gilbert and then Rick Steiner to gain the titles.

But in 1987, when the UWF started to book matches with the more established NWA, Sting began to really stick out. He went onto the solo's circuit where he was very successful. The UWF and NWA would eventually merge and the federation officials not only liked the way Sting wrestled in the ring, they liked the attention he was getting from the crowd when he went up against prominent grapplers like the then NWA U.S. champion Lex Luger. Sting was climbing up the wrestling ladder pretty quickly and would soon find wrestling legend Ric Flair waiting for him at the top, ready to grapple.

There would be no more toying around on the mid-card. Sting had moved up to main event status almost immediately. The hype of the match between the legend and the newcomer lasted a couple of weeks, then finally, in February 1988, Flair and Sting clashed in an all-out battle that left the fans craving for more. Even though the still-green grappler lost to the veteran wrestler, Sting managed to impress the audience and proved that he meant serious business.

Though Flair came away with the victory that night, he also had to be carried out of the ring on a stretcher. Sting got him into his scorpion hold during the contest and didn't let go of the helpless Flair for almost three minutes.

The two tangled again one month later, on March 27, 1998, at the Clash of the Champions match. This, too, was a memorable night for Sting, as he again put on a great show for the fans and also gained the respect of his legendary opponent. He went the forty-five-minute distance with him in this time-limited confrontation.

Flair and Sting went at each other in this battle with everything in their arsenals, but the match still ended in a draw. Flair used his years of ring experience, bag of dirty tricks and his famous figure-four lock on his young opponent, while Sting went at him with high-flying maneuvers, stinger splashes, speed and his extremely dangerous and painful scorpion move. And yet the war ended with no victor.

Sting was now quickly making friends with the NWA fans, but he was also quickly making enemies with his fellow grapplers on the circuit. Many wrestlers were getting jealous of the young mat-man who was stealing their limelight and fans, a jealousy that trickled over into the ring. He was not only becoming extremely popular in his first two years in the federation; he was also becoming a marked man.

He combined briefly with Lex Luger to do battle with the Road Warriors, then gained his first single's title when he defeated Mike Rotunda in March 1989, earning the right to be called World Television title holder. At this time, Ric Flair was out to get the young Stinger, because Ric and his henchmen, "the Four Horsemen," were constantly doing battle with him. As if Flair and his posse weren't enough trouble, the Great Muta would also arrive on the scene and want a piece of the federation's newcomer.

Muta, who was coming off a great wrestling run in Japan, proved to be a great matchup with Sting. He combined aerial acrobatics with martial arts and also shot a colored liquid from his mouth, rendering his opponents momentarily blind.

The two finally clashed in January 1989 at the Great American Bash, and the fans weren't disappointed. Sting countered his opponent's arsenal with his own bag of tricks and exited the ring with what he thought would be a title victory. But the championship was taken away because during their match, Muta accidentally sprayed the original referee in the eye with his illegal red dye and the ref was replaced with an alternate. Even though Sting legally won the match, the TV title was now declared vacant because of the antics that went on in the ring.

That night Sting again clashed with Muta, as the Japanese sensation interfered in the World Title match between Flair and Terry Funk. Sting came to the aid of his former foe Flair and they joined forces before the end of the night to form an awesome duo.

Sting would officially lose his title that year to Muta, but would team with Flair in a Thunderdome Cage Match at 1989's Halloween Havoc and get revenge on his opponent and Funk. Sting and Flair would punish the two grapplers inside a steel cage in a match that was both memorable and vicious. Muta would be rendered helpless after a painful crotch shot, and Funk would fall victim to a Sting/Flair double team, as Flair held Funk in a figure-four while Sting punished him from above the top rope.

The duo seemed unbeatable and there was even talk that Sting might join the Horsemen. In 1989 at Starrcade, Sting emerged victorious in an Iron-Man Tournament, where he took on and beat several different wrestlers to get to the finals of the tourney. In the finals, he squared off against Flair and beat his tag partner for the Iron-Man crown. Thinking that his World Title would be in danger, Flair again offered Sting the chance to become a Horseman and he accepted, but this union would only last a short while.

The NWA scheduled Sting and Flair to face off at a title tilt at WrestleWar in 1990 with the World Strap on the line. When the Horsemen told Sting to decline acceptance of the title opportunity match and show them loyalty, he became outraged and tried to attack Flair. His attack was foiled by the "Four Henchmen" and he was not only unable to take part in the title-shot match, he would also be out of action for six months with a knee injury, thanks to the brutal beating from the foursome.

Lex Luger was now granted the title shot against Flair. Sting would appear at ringside to cheer his former opponent on against his dirty ex-partner. Just when Luger had Flair right where he wanted him (he had Flair in his torture-rack finisher), Arn and Ole Anderson attacked Sting at ringside, causing Luger to drop Flair and run to the aid of his friend. While he was helping Sting, he was counted out of the ring by the ref and Flair remained the champ.

In July 1990, Sting was fit and ready to challenge Flair for the belt. The two met at the Great American Bash. It was an awesome battle, with each wrestler applying immense pressure on his opponent; but in the end, The Stinger would finally come away victorious. Flair, who was trying to apply his famous figure-four lock for the win, was caught off-guard by Sting when the young, face-painted wrestler caught him with an inside cradle and scored the victory for the NWA World Title.

In a classy move, Sting paid homage to his beaten opponent when he said in a postmatch interview: "Ric Flair is the greatest World champion of all time. I am champion for one night and one night only because I have some big shoes to fill."

The Venice Beach native would prove to be a good champion and would hold the title for a while through battles with Flair, Sid Vicious and many newcomers who came onto the mat scene. One of the newcomers was truly an unknown to wrestling fans, officials and Sting as he came to the ring in a mask and called himself the

Black Scorpion. The Scorpion claimed to know Sting from his earlier days on the left coast and wanted a title challenge for old time's
sake.

The story line lasted for quite some time and came to a halt at
Starrcade 1990 when the Stinger met the Black Scorpion in a steel-
cage match. While he squared off against this masked foe, four
more masked villains appeared at cage-side and it was quite obvious who was under the mask battling Sting in the ring. When he
scored the pin on his mysterious foe, he pulled the mask off to
reveal to the audience who his opponent was—none other than Ric
Flair. (Even though it wasn't really Flair under the mask each time
The Black Scorpion squared off against Sting, fans were supposed
to believe that it was.) Flair would meet Sting less than one month
later and would win back the title he had originally lost to his foe in
July at the American Bash.

Nineteen ninety-one would be a big year for both Sting and his
federation. The wrestler's next stop would be the tag ranks, where
he teamed with Lex Luger against the Steiner Brothers at Super-
Brawl, while the NWA was being transformed into the WCW by the
wrestling organization's new boss Ted Turner. Turner planned on
airing his product on his cable station (TNT), in direct competition
with Vince McMahon's WWF promotion, which aired on the USA
network.

Speaking of competition, Sting and Luger would have defeated
the brothers at the 1991 SuperBrawl, but Nikita Koloff came in and
interfered in the match. Koloff was about to hit Luger with one of
his infamous Russian Sickles when Sting came in and took the full
force of the blow. Taking advantage when Sting was down on the
mat, Scott Steiner pinned his opponent for the tainted win.

Sting may have let the Steiners walk away with the victory, but he didn't let Koloff get away so easily. He was so pissed that Koloff was allowed to interfere in the tag match that he attacked the Russian grappler after the bout. This would be the first of many encounters between the two heavyweight wrestlers.

When the Koloff angle became played out, he turned his energies to the vacant WCW U.S. title. The title became vacant when Lex Luger won the World Title, and had to give up the U.S. belt. As a result, the federation was now holding a tournament to see who would be the next holder of the number one contender's strap.

Sting was in top form during the tourney, and he beat Arn Anderson, Diamond Studd and "Stunning" Steve Austin for the right not only to be the new U.S. champion, but also for the number one contender's ranking for the heavyweight title.

But a funny thing happened on the way to the number one ranking—actually, several funny things began to happen. At one WCW Saturday Night, Sting received a very large gift box, which just happened to contain the wrestler Abdullah the Butcher. The prized wrestler proceeded to attack the face-painted grappler. He would receive another gift box after his victory over Johnny B. Badd at Clash of Champions, and this time Cactus Jack would attack Sting but, unlike the first incident, Sting was prepared and was able to defend himself.

The "generous" gift-givers turned out to be The Dangerous Alliance (Paul E. Dangerously and Rick Rude), who wanted to get Rude a shot at Sting's U.S. Title. The gimmick worked—Rude got a shot at the belt and won it with a little help from Lex Luger, who attacked and hurt Sting on purpose before his match began, thus giving Rude an edge.

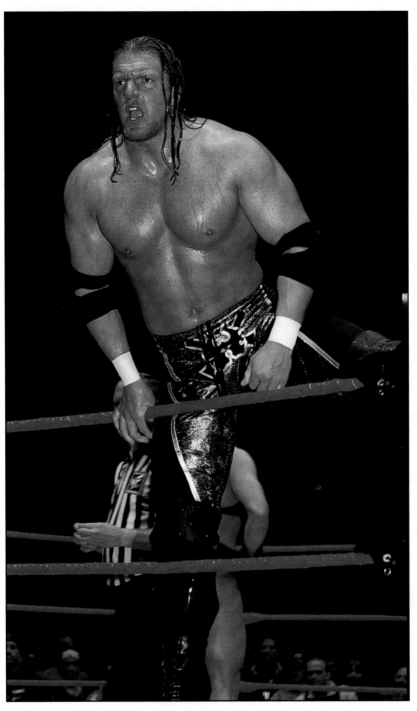

No ring can contain the fury of Triple H.

J&E Sports Photography

Sid Vicious prepares to lay the Powerbomb on an unfortunate foe.

J&E Sports Photography

The Undertaker shows his dark side—the only one he has!

J&E Sports Photography

Diamond Dallas Page
wants opponents to
"feel the bang"!

R. Grabowski

Scott Hall does
things his way.

R. Grabowski

All of Chris Jericho's enemies have the Y2J problem.

R. Grabowski

It's all a wild downward spiral when Edge is in the ring.

J&E Sports Photography

Buff Bagwell has the right stuff to make the audience go nuts!

J&E Sports Photography

Big Vito and Johnny the Bull (aka Mamalukes) send a rival to sleep with the fishes.

R. Grabowski

The Godfather certainly makes "pimpin'" look easy
alongside his "ho's"!

J&E Sports Photography

Sparks are sure to fly when Goldberg enters the ring.

R. Grabowski

At Starrcade 1991 Sting got even with both of these dirty wrestlers. He participated in BattleBowl, which was a battle royal where several wrestlers took part. He was pitted in one match against Rude, whom he would have some problems with, but eventually came out on top. In the finals he met up with Lex Luger, where he also got sweet revenge.

The taste of revenge would become even sweeter, as he was now again officially ranked number one contender and would square off against Luger in February at SuperBrawl II. Sting not only beat Luger in this Milwaukee event, he pulverized and abused his former friend throughout the entire match, ending it with a flying-body press to take his first World Title.

He held onto his title for five months, until Big Van Vader took the strap away. He and Vader had been clashing for several months and the feud came to an all-time high when Vader powerslammed Sting to the mat that April, causing him to crack two ribs and bruise his spleen. This would keep the Stinger out of action for quite some time.

All healed and ready, he would return with only Vader and revenge on his mind. Sting would win a couple of tune-up matches before he was to meet the big guy again in the ring. The two finally clashed on July 12, 1992, at the Great American Bash at the Beach, and, surprisingly, Sting lost the match and belt to Vader.

Sting was supposed to have a rematch with Vader in August with the title on the line once again, but due to an unfortunate incident involving Jake "The Snake" Roberts, Sting had to forfeit his shot at the title, and his chance was now given to Ron Simmons. (Simmons would take advantage of the opportunity and defeat Vader, to become the first African American Heavyweight Champion in WCW history.) Roberts had attacked Sting one night when he came to the aid of Nikita Koloff, who was being double-teamed by Rick Rude and Cactus Jack.

"I've been attacked from behind by everyone from Jake 'The Snake' Roberts to Cactus Jack, but I always get my revenge," the steamed wrestler said.

This uncalled-for attack started a feud between Sting and The Snake that would last until that year's Halloween Havoc. Once this feud was over, Sting would turn his concentration back to becoming the WCW's number one contender so he could get back the heavyweight belt. This would also revive another rivalry from his past, Big Van Vader.

In order to get a shot at the number one slot, he would have to enter the King of Cable Tournament. Sting proceeded to enter the event and did away with whoever was thrown in front of him. He first knocked off Brian Pillman and then he beat up on another old foe, Rick Rude. He next faced Vader in the finals, and after a hard-fought battle, beat his four-hundred-pound opponent, thus becoming the federation's number one contender.

The story only gets better. Two days after his loss to Sting, Vader would regain the WCW Heavyweight Championship from Ron Simmons, which heated up his feud with his long-time rival. The two would bump heads on many occasions over the next couple of months, but one of the best battles occurred at SuperBrawl III in a Strap Match. In the end, Vader retained his title over Sting, but would leave severely battered and bruised. Big Van would have to be hospitalized, as he sustained a lacerated back and ruptured artery in his ear.

In March, the two battlers would have it out twice overseas. The first match happened on March 11, 1993, in England, where Sting would record the victory over Vader and capture his second Heavyweight Championship. But Vader got the last laugh on foreign soil, as he recaptured the belt six days later in Dublin, Ireland.

The rest of 1993 had Sting still battling the round mound of wrestling, but he would also clash with another Titan, Sid Vicious, for a while. These feuds were nothing to brag about but they kept him occupied until Hulk Hogan arrived on the scene in 1994. While all the WCW fans were foaming at the mouth for a Hogan/Sting battle to take place, this wouldn't be the case for some time. As a matter of fact, the first time the two would even appear in the ring together was when Sting came to the defense of the Hulkster at the 1994 Halloween Havoc, when Hogan, after a cage match with Ric Flair, was being outnumbered by Flair, The Butcher, Kevin Sullivan and Avalanche.

The two wouldn't square off in a match until one year after Hogan's arrival. During a Monday Nitro broadcast on November 20, 1995, Sting would wrestle the former WWF champ. He would mock Hogan by coming into the ring dressed in the Hulkster's red and yellow colors—with matching face paint, to boot!

The match lived up to its billing, and the only disappointment was that there was no winner. It ended in a DQ just when it looked as Sting would come away with the victory, because the Dungeon of Doom interfered in the monster bash.

From here on in, Sting would not only battle Hogan, but he would also do battle with Hulk's newly formed gang—the nWo. Sting was out to stop this group, who wanted to take over the federation and turn the wrestlers against the WCW. After a while it seemed Sting was fighting a battle he couldn't win, as grappler after grappler started to move over to the dark side.

But he would stop fighting his WCW cause when his loyalty was questioned. Two weeks before the 1996 WarGames, Lex Luger was attacked by someone who looked like Sting and rumors began to circulate that he had changed allegiances. When it was later proven to the doubters that the assailant wasn't Sting but a look-alike, the real Sting was too hurt to forgive his accusers. At WarGames, Sting turned away from the WCW. On the following night on a Nitro telecast, he appeared like no one had seen him before.

Instead of his usual blond crew cut and multicolored face paint, Sting was now a dead ringer for Brandon Lee's character from the movie *The Crow*, dressed in all black, with a white-painted face and carrying a black bat. Sting's new character went over well with the fans and made him even more popular than in his early wrestling days.

His new image appeared on posters, T-shirts and many other wrestling-related items that were selling out in Hulkamanialike proportions. Speaking of the Hulk, Sting would again clash in the ring with him in the December 1997 Starrcade, and this time there would be a winner (or would there?), as the Stinger beat the future Hall of Fame grappler and claimed his third WCW World Heavy-weight title.

The win was a controversial one, because first Hogan thought he had the victory when the ref gave him a quick three-count on Sting; but Bret Hart came to Sting's defense and knocked out the ref in the process, allowing the fight to continue. Sting would then get his opponent in a Scorpion Deathlock, and Hogan gave in to Sting for the win.

On January 8, 1998, Sting's title was declared vacant due to his controversial match with Hogan in December, and he had to clash with the Hulkster once again if he wanted the championship. On February 22, the two megastars clashed at SuperBrawl in San Francisco with the belt on the line, and Sting came out on top again for his fourth world title.

He lost the belt two months later, however, to Randy Savage in Denver, and stepped away from wrestling for a while due to what he deemed "personal business." He returned to the mat in April 1999 and garnered his fifth world title, defeating Diamond Dallas Page in a WCW event in Fargo, North Dakota.

Sting had no time to enjoy this victory, as a Four-Corners Match was concocted on that same night and the five-time champ would have to square off against DDP, Kevin Nash and Goldberg and defend his belt. He made it to the finals of this match against DDP, but wound up losing the belt in the end.

It would take the Stinger five months to get back to the top of the WCW's championship mountain. He met and beat Hulk Hogan on September 12, 1999, in Winston-Salem for his sixth World Heavyweight title, but was stripped of his crown one month later for "assaulting" referee Charles Robinson.

Announcers and fans questioned his violent actions on the "helpless" ref at the time, but with that incident behind him and six titles to his credit, the only question left is, Where does Sting go from here?

"Wrestling is the greatest thing that's ever happened to me," Sting said. "It gives me the opportunity to make good money, be recognized, see the world and stay in good physical condition. I don't know what more anyone could ask for?"

How about a seventh title?

Triple H

REAL NAME: **Jean-Paul Levesque**

HEIGHT: **6'4"**

WEIGHT: **246 lbs.**

BIRTHPLACE: **Greenwich, Connecticut**

FINISHING MOVE: **The Pedigree**

FAVORITE QUOTE: **"Let's get ready to . . . suck it!"**

TRIPLE H (Hunter Hearst Helmsley), a.k.a. Jean-Paul LeVesque, is a three-time WWF champion, but he may very well be the most-hated title holder. As a matter of fact, during his most recent reign, modern technology almost stripped him of his championship, as wrestling fans from all over the world were E-mailing the WWF headquarters demanding that Helmsley be stripped of the strap immediately. They wanted to see the people's champion, The Rock, sitting on the WWF throne, and they almost got their way. The federation's front office had a powwow to discuss the situation and ultimately decided to leave Triple H as champ.

They realized that even though this guy was truly hated by the loyal watchers, it made great sense in business and for the story line to leave him where he was. He was getting the fans to react and interact, and that's a big part of the sports entertainment business—reaction.

The normal reaction nowadays when Triple H enters a building is anything *but* normal. As a matter of fact, it's pretty harsh when twenty thousand crazy fans are chanting "asshole, asshole!" But the Heavyweight Champion doesn't mind being the federation's most popular heel.

"Things change so fast around here," Triple H explained. "I like where I'm at now. I foresee myself as being, and trying to be, and hopefully continuing to be the number one heel in this business—the most hated guy in the business. That suits me just fine."

However, he also realizes that he may be losing out a little in other areas of the business, namely financially and popularity-wise; but he takes it all in stride and rolls with the punches.

"I sometimes think I'm an idiot for doing it," he said. "As a heel in the business you make less money because of royalties, which [I believe] is wrong. You get less fanfare, you get less publicity outside of the business, you get less push by the office [and] you get less respect all around." But turning heel has put him back on top of the federation, where he believes he'll remain for a long time, and for that he's grateful.

"I like being a heel much more," he said. "I think I'm better at it. . . . I'm one of the very few guys left in this business who is willing to get legitimate heat (for being bad). . . . I think a lot of guys in our business want to be heels a lot of times because the heel sometimes is a more interesting character. You get to do more dastardly stuff, so sometimes it's more fun. But they want to do it in such a way that the fans still think they're cool."

But Triple H, on the other hand, couldn't care less. As a matter of fact, the six-foot-four grappler would probably hit all those fans who didn't think he was cool with an ever-popular D-Generation X catchphrase and tell them to "suck it!"

LeVesque has made a lucrative career out of being an unpopular wrestling personality. He first got started in the business in 1992 when he trained with the Hall of Fame grappler Killer Kowalski. Being a quick learner and well-conditioned athlete, he made his professional debut as Terra Ryzing only two months later in March for Kowalski in a New England independent federation, the IWF. Not long after his debut, LeVesque would win his first championship belt when he beat Mad Dog Richard for the IWF Heavyweight Championship belt.

He toiled in the indies for two short years before World Championship Wrestling came knocking at his front door and offered him a tryout. The Greenwich, Connecticut, native jumped at the opportunity and packed his bags and Ryzing persona and headed to Atlanta.

Having impressed the powers that be at the time in WCW, LeVesque inked a contract with the federation and was welcomed to the big time by being put into a feud with fan favorite Johnny B. Badd. Even though Badd dominated the matches against Ryzing, it was good for the federation rookie to get his feet wet.

A short while later, he would make and win his TV debut match against Brian Armstrong. Although they liked his potential, the WCW didn't like the Ryzing character or name, so they scratched that personality and used his last name, LeVesque. The LeVesque character was to be a wealthy, cultivated, arrogant and snooty French Canadian grappler with a babyface. But the LeVesque gimmick never got off the ground—he only appeared in one Pay-Per-View, the 1994 Starrcade, where he lost to Alex Wright. LeVesque began to question not only the direction his character was going in, but also his future in the WCW.

Feeling neglected, the 246-pound wrestler explored his options and soon found interest from the other major federation, the WWF. He left the WCW and what he considered their broken promises behind and moved back home to Connecticut where, coincidentally, his new federation's offices were located.

Looking for a clean start in his new federation, LeVesque decided to go with a new ring name. He chose Hunter Hearst Helmsley as his moniker. The personality would have all the lowest characteristics of the wealthy—the greediness, the cockiness, the designer clothes and of course, the wealth. He chose the "Hearst" part of his name in tribute to the egotistical billionaire William Randolph Hearst and the "Helmsley" part was taken from Leona Helmsley, the stuffy millionaire heiress of the Helmsley hotel fortune. He was putting himself into a character whom fans were going to love to hate, but again he didn't mind as long as he got some kind of feedback from the crowd.

Hunter made his WWF debut in July 1995 against Henry Godwin. This was a great matchup, since opposites not only attract, but also provide some good wrestling. The Godwin character was your typical farmer, minus the good country boy looks! The baseball-cap-wearing Godwin would mosey on into the ring unshaven with his overalls covering his beer belly, while Helmsley would strut his way to the mat with his clean-shaven babyface looks, stylish black rider's pants and chiseled physique. This battle with the former hard-working hog farmer would be the first of Helmsley's many battles with the WWF's blue-collar grapplers.

The snobby wrestler began to catch on with both the male and female fans. The men would look forward to watching him wrestle because of his arrogance and skill in between the ropes (and the fact that he was always accompanied to the ring by one of several beautiful valets didn't hurt), while the women loved him for his long blond locks, handsome face and muscular body (and the fact that his character came from money probably came into play, too).

One of the best stories to come out of his persona and ring entrances involved his most famous valet, Rena Mero, known to all wrestling fans as Sable. The gorgeous blond would accompany Helmsley to the ring for matches, and when he lost he would take his losses out on her in front of the crowd. What "The Greenwich Snob" didn't know was that his berating Sable in public would not only cause him to lose the beautiful valet, it would also set the stage for a feud between him and newcomer "Wildman" Marc Mero, who also just happened to be her real-life husband.

At WrestleMania XII, Helmsley took on the Ultimate Warrior and lost in embarrassing fashion (one minute and forty-three seconds) to the grappler who had been away from the federation for some time. When he blamed his valet for the loss to The Warrior, Mero came to her defense.

"The Wildman" Mero grew tired of watching HHH treat Sable terribly, so he turned on the charm and won her over to his corner to be his valet and together they formed one of the sport's best one-two punches. At the time. Helmsley watched his former valet guide Mero to an Intercontinental Championship, which added more fuel to the fire of this feud that lasted until the end of 1996.

During his feud with Mero, many were questioning whether or not HHH had what it takes to wrestle with the big boys. Helmsley would beat the trunks off any of the lower-card talent he would face in the ring, but he just wasn't having that type of luck or success when he squared off against the Razor Ramons and Bret Harts of the wrestling world.

Just when it looked like HHH was being lost in the shuffle, he hooked on with a WWF grappling group known as "The Kliq." Being associated with the likes of Shawn Michaels, Diesel (Kevin Nash) and Razor Ramon (Scott Hall) did wonders for his career at this time because The Kliq seemed to get special treatment from Vince McMahon. The WWF boss allowed them to have a say in which wrestlers were going to get a push and which ones were going to be buried.

This was great while it lasted, but it would come back to haunt him some time later as Helmsley became the fall guy for the Kliq members, who one night acted out of character in the ring. It was an incident that McMahon deemed disrespectful to his federation.

On May 19, 1996, in New York's Madison Square Garden, the fans witnessed the final matches Razor Ramon and Diesel wrestled for the WWF, because the two had inked deals with the rival federation, WCW, which would go into effect when their WWF contracts expired. Well, the contracts just happened to terminate on the nineteenth, the night of this Madison Square Garden event, so let's just say that the members of The Kliq decided to throw a "Garden" party that night and not only celebrated at the end of the night amongst themselves in the ring, but they also included twenty thousand screaming fans in on the good-bye to Ramon and Diesel.

The reason this was so wrong was that they broke character in front of the fans. That is a no-no in the biz because the fans are supposed to believe that these superstars are really who they are in the ring. They are not supposed to stray away from their character's story lines, especially if they just wrestled against one another.

"There was a strong bond between us and it being Kevin and Scott's last stand, it was a very emotional night for all of us," HHH explained.

Well, McMahon obviously couldn't punish Ramon or Diesel, since they were no longer his to discipline and he wasn't going to take it out on his meal ticket at the time, Shawn Michaels, so he decided to make an example of Helmsley. He got buried for a couple of months by the federation and the King of the Ring title he was supposed to win was instead won by Steve Austin.

When Helmsley was asked about the incident and about losing the chance at winning the title, he said: "Do I regret the incident? Emotionally no, [but] from a business standpoint maybe just a tiny bit."

But what transpired next in Helmsley's career should go down in the heel hall of fame. HHH hired Curt Hennig, who had been absent from the WWF for three years, as his manager. Hennig and Helmsley plotted to pull off one of the best scams in federation history.

The two made everyone believe that the partnership that they had formed was beginning to fall apart, as Hennig began escorting

Helmsley's female valets from ringside after matches. Appearing to be irate, HHH challenged Hennig to a match on a Monday Night RAW. The contest turned out to be a hoax. Helmsley appeared to attack Hennig before the match and Hennig faked being injured and claimed he couldn't compete that night. His friend, Marc Mero, then offered to fill in for the injured wrestler.

Helmsley agreed to tangle with the "The Wildman," but only if Mero would put his Intercontinental strap on the line. "The Wildman" agreed to the terms and Helmsley defeated him for his first WWF title. Mero was livid after the bout when he found out that the two grapplers had plotted all along to dethrone him.

From there, Helmsley moved on to another dastardly deed when he tried to pry one of his fellow wrestler's (Goldust) manager, Marlena, out from under his nose. Although he wasn't successful at doing this, HHH did manage to defend his IC title against the WWF's gold wonder with the help of his butler Curtis Hughes. Unfortunately, Hughes didn't last too long by Helmsley's side because he had to leave the federation due to health problems. In the meantime, Hunter was trying to convince Vince McMahon to bring over one of his female bodybuilder friends, Joanie Laurer (Chyna), into the WWF so she could become his private bodyguard.

McMahon finally gave in and HHH brought in his friend, who would watch his back while he was in the ring. Helmsley's bodybuilder friend was none other than the Ninth Wonder of the World—Chyna. Chyna immediately showed the fans and wrestling world what she had by pummeling Marlena for her boss during one of his matches, as Marlena tried to interfere in one of Triple H's bouts.

In February 1997, HHH lost his next IC title defense at an In-

Your-House event to a freshman grappler who was trying to make a name for himself at the time—Rocky Maivia. Even though he lost the title, he still remained focused and eventually won another championship—he was the victor of that year's King of the Ring tournament against Mankind (Mick Foley). This would be the start of a long feud between him and Foley (a.k.a. Mankind, Cactus Jack and Dude Love).

In December he also gained another title, when he "defeated" Shawn Michaels in a clown match to win the European title. The reason this match was so funny was that Michaels set up Helmsley to win because WWF commissioner Sgt. Slaughter wanted him to defend his title, so he chose his friend. HHH got the easy pin and was awarded the belt.

Upon winning the Euro title, Helmsley would now start a rivalry with Owen Hart. He would lose this title to Hart, but not by fault of his own. Even though he was injured, the WWF officials still wanted him to defend his strap. Hunter proceeded to send the artist formerly known as Goldust to the ring disguised as HHH to compete against Hart. The plan would backfire on HHH, as Hart won and Goldust lost his title, even though HHH really didn't wrestle.

Helmsley met up with Hart in March at a RAW IS WAR and regained his belt and European title. He held onto the strap for another four months until D'Lo Brown took it from him with a little help from The Rock, on July 14, 1998.

Soon after on a RAW IS WAR, he was forced to team with Shawn "The Heartbreak Kid" Michaels in a tag match against Mankind and Steve Austin. The pairing seemed to inspire the two former Kliq members to reunite and form another group . . . for old time's sake. The new group, or gang as it was later labeled, was called D-Generation X. The charter posse members consisted of Michaels, Helmsley, Chyna and the late Rick Rude.

The gang was known for their rule-breaking, crotch-chopping gestures, match interferences, crowd mooning and cursing on national TV. Although Michaels fought most of the group's battles, HHH's role down the road would increase tremendously as The Heartbreak Kid had to take some time off to recuperate from a major injury. Many questioned whether or not Triple H could lead the group. Needless to say, he not only succeeded, but thrived under the pressure!

After recruiting some new members and adding some comedy skits to their usual shtick, Helmsley had DX where it never had been before—in the limelight. Not only were the fans nuts about this rule-breaking gang, they were also making the members rich. DX merchandise was second in sales only to Steve Austin paraphernalia. It was during this time that Triple H also came out with the Michael Buffer–like saying, "Let's get ready to . . . suck it!"

The gang theme was at its best when DX battled another WWF group, the Nation of Domination. This not only led to great group brawls, but also awesome individual action, when Triple H would square off against the Nation's leader, The Rock. One of the best matches between the two occurred during a 1998 SummerSlam ladder match, where Triple H regained his IC title. In October, he would be forced to relinquish this belt because he was unable to defend his title due to an injury.

Over the next part of his career, there would be many interesting events involving Triple H. For example, he turned his back on DX and aligned with Shane McMahon. Also, who could forget the clips of him marrying a passed-out Stephanie McMahon in Vegas in

November? But there was nothing more satisfying for the blond bomber than when he won his first-ever World Championship on August 23, 1999. Triple H beat Mankind on a RAW IS WAR for the right to wear the cherished belt. But less than one month later, he lost the title to his boss, Vince McMahon, who had some assistance from Stone Cold Steve Austin.

Ten days later, Triple H had the belt on his mind as he was to compete in an UNFORGIVEN event in a six-pack match, where the winner would be crowned WWF champ. When all was said and done he would defeat The Rock, Mankind, The Big Show, Kane and the British Bulldog for his second championship. He would again lose it less than one month later (on November 14, 1999), this time to The Big Show in a Triple Threat match.

Not one to hang his head, Triple H went about his business for the next month and a half until his time came around for another shot at the belt. He started the new year off with a bang as he was crowned WWF champ for the third time on January 3, 2000. He now deemed himself not only federation champion, but also "The Game!"

At WrestleMania XVI in Anaheim, California, Triple H successfully defended his crown in a Fatal Four-Way match against The Rock, Cactus Jack and The Big Show. "The Game" did not play fair in the championship match, as he was aided by his "father-in-law," Vince McMahon, in his win. But in the end it doesn't matter how you play—as long as you win.

Triple H always preached to his competitors, "I am the Hunter and everyone else is the Hunted." But ironically, "The Game" has changed, as he is now "the Hunted." But that's the price one has to pay if they want to be the WWF Heavyweight Champion.

Heat Generators

WRESTLING characters not only come in many shapes and sizes, but they also have many different roles to play throughout their careers. One of these roles is to be a Heat Generator—somebody who stirs up the pot and keeps things interesting.

These troublemakers can be either babyfaces or heels, rookies or veterans. There is no set formula. Hell, in some instances they can even be the boss's son or daughter! Any way you slice it, the Heat Generators make wrestling more exciting. They get fans going and can be counted upon to appear at every event.

Take a look at some of the superstars who are currently mixing it up in their federation. You may be surprised to find out who made this stirring list!

RIC FLAIR

HEIGHT: **6'1"**
WEIGHT: **243 lbs.**
HOMETOWN: **Minneapolis, Minnesota**
FINISHING MOVE: **Figure-Four Lock**

To be the man, you have to beat this man! This veteran grappler has been around the pro wrestling ring for twenty-eight years and there seems to be no slowing him down.

Just when you think you saw the last of the stylin' and profilin' wrestler, he shows up and immediately gets involved in the mix. Ric Flair is not only an excellent athlete who is the proud owner of thirteen world championships; he can also be considered a trendsetter in the business, given that he was one of the first grapplers to form a wrestling posse. In May 1986 he formed The Four Horsemen, who set the precedent for other hell-raising gangs like D-X, The nWo, The Radicals, The Brood, The Flock and many, many others.

The Nature Boy has done battle in the ring with Hulk Hogan, Sting, Diamond Dallas Page, Randy Savage, Dusty Rhodes, Roddy Piper and countless others over his illustrious career. Even at age fifty-one, there seems to be no end to what this master matsman can do! "Whooooooo!"

THE UNDERTAKER

HEIGHT: **6'10"**
WEIGHT: **328 lbs.**
HOMETOWN: **Death Valley**
FINISHING MOVE: **Tombstone Piledriver**

Darth Vader has nothing on this WWF dark warrior, who has been stirring up trouble ever since his federation debut at the 1990 Survivor Series. Before being sidelined with an injury in 1999, he had teamed with another "Giant"-sized wrestler, The Big Show, promising to bring about armageddon in the World Wrestling Federation.

The Undertaker is the proud owner of three World Heavyweight titles, plus three tag-team straps, and doesn't plan on stopping there. The former leader of the Ministry of Darkness isn't afraid to mix it up with anybody. He has clashed not only with his own brother, Kane, in the ring, but also with the man who signs his paychecks, Vince McMahon.

God help the federation when the frightening 'Taker comes back from the dead. They should be afraid. Very afraid!

JEFF JARRETT

HEIGHT: **5'10"**
WEIGHT: **230 lbs.**
HOMETOWN: **Nashville, Tennessee**
FINISHING MOVE: **The Stroke**

Grapplers are finding out the hard way not to piss off Jeff Jarrett (also called Double J), as one by one they are coming down with headaches after taking a guitar to the noggin from wrestling's version of the cartoon character El Kabong!

This second-generation bruiser made his pro debut in 1986 on the indie circuit when he stepped between the ropes for his dad's Memphis promotion. In short order, he recorded an impressive record of twenty-five championships while working for the small organizations like the CWA and the USWA.

From there he moved on to the WWF, where he would make his big-time debut in 1994. Double J climbed the success ladder rather quickly in his first tour of duty in the federation, when he garnered the Intercontinental title in his first year as a pro on January 22, 1995. The instrument-swinging wrestler jumped from big promotion to big promotion, and in the process would win another eight championship belts (seven WWF and one WCW).

Don't expect Jarrett to record any musical hits with his guitar in the near future. The only hits Double J will be making are the ones over his opponents heads, because he's a swinger, not a singer!

KANE

HEIGHT: 7'0"
WEIGHT: 326 lbs.
HOMETOWN: Death Valley
FINISHING MOVE: The Tombstone Piledriver

This monster in the ring can generate heat with the best of 'em! He literally burst on the WWF scene in 1997, when he tore off the cage door during an October Hell in the Cell match to get at his brother The Undertaker.

From there all hell surely broke loose in the wrestling world, as Kane thought nothing of demolishing any grappler who was in his way, especially his "older brother." There certainly was no brotherly love between the two siblings when Kane first came onto the federation scene. He would constantly challenge his brother, but The Undertaker wanted no part of a contest against his younger brother.

The two would eventually square off at WrestleMania XIV in a memorable tilt, where the two fought under the flames of an Inferno Match. Less than one year later, the Big Red Machine would win his first-ever WWF championship against "Stone Cold" Steve Austin in a title match at the 1998 King of the Ring. The mean grappler would also capture the tag straps three times in his career, winning the belts on two separate occasions with Mankind and once with X-Pac.

This defiant, seven-foot wrestler has proven that he is afraid of anyone, and that he will do whatever it takes to get what he wants— namely, the WWF championship. Kane has the ability both to pulverize and scare his opponents at any given moment and because of that the sky—or the underground—is the limit for this scary superstar.

SCOTT HALL

HEIGHT: **6'5"**
WEIGHT: **280 lbs.**
HOMETOWN: **Miami, Florida**
FINISHING MOVE: **Outsider's Edge**

Scott Hall is a renegade from the word go. No one tells this guy what to do—he has a mind of his own. The outlaw grappler can't be told anything; not how to wrestle, not who to wrestle, not where to go—as a matter of fact, *he's* the one constantly telling people where to go!

In mid-1992 Scott Hall made his mark in the wrestling world by introducing the Razor Ramon character to the WWF fans. The greased-back hair, slick wrestling maneuvers, cocky attitude and toothpick dangling from his mouth all made this wrestler into a rebel with a cause. And his cause is simply to wreak havoc on whatever federation he is in at the time.

Over the course of his rebellious career in both the WWF and WCW, Hall has won five singles titles and five tag titles (all with Kevin Nash) and has also been a part of numerous "Kliqs" in his career, the two most famous being the Outsiders and the nWo.

Hall has the ability to get under people's skin and turn things topsy-turvy, but more important, this Florida native has the ability to win wrestling matches.

SHANE McMAHON

HEIGHT: **6'2"**

WEIGHT: **230 lbs.**

HOMETOWN: **Greenwich, Connecticut**

FINISHING MOVE: **Clobbering opponents with foreign objects**

Why does Shane McMahon get away with anything he wants to in the WWF? Not because he's the boss's son. No, no, no. It's more because he knows how to pick his allies—and also when to abandon them.

His first smart maneuver was to align himself with The Undertaker and form one of the most horrifying factions ever to hit the World Wrestling Federation. The Corporate Ministry was a mean, sadistic bunch who took no crap from anyone, including his father, the senior McMahon.

The ruthless attitude he picked up while being a part of the Ministry has carried over into his in-ring persona, and has also led to his winning the European championship over X-Pac on February 15, 1999, in Birmingham, Alabama.

The heir apparent to the WWF kingdom admits to being born with a silver spoon in his mouth, but he also dares anyone to try and knock it out. The smart grapplers will stay away from that challenge because it's a battle they won't be able to win, even if they do succeed in taking the utensil from Shane's mouth.

The ignorant wrestlers are the ones who will be banished to the WCW for not only going over the boss's head, but for going after it!

LEX LUGER

HEIGHT: **6'4"**
WEIGHT: **265 lbs.**
HOMETOWN: **Chicago, Illinois**
FINISHING MOVE: **The Torture Rack**

Lex Luger is living proof that good looks will get you anywhere. This chiseled grappler made his pro debut on October 31, 1985, and is still going strong fifteen years later.

"The Total Package" has worn many different championship belts in his successful career on the mat. During his time with World Championship Wrestling, he has held each of their most prestigious titles—the U.S. Heavyweight, Tag Team, TV and World Heavyweight—twice, and was showing no signs of slowing down.

Luger should have had many, many more straps in his showcase, but was always the victim of a screw job in the big matches. Nowadays, he has taken matters into his own hands, as he always has a can of mace, his trusty black bat and his manipulative sidekick, Elizabeth, at ringside.

At one time or another, "The Package" was aligned with several different wrestling affiliations (The Four Horsemen, The Allied Powers, The Dungeon of Doom, nWo Wolfpac and the New World Order), who made life difficult for other wrestlers.

But today he seems content with raising hell by himself!

THE BIG SHOW

HEIGHT: **7'2"**
WEIGHT: **500 lbs.**
HOMETOWN: **Tampa, Florida**
FINISHING MOVE: **The Showstopper**

The World Wrestling Federation's seven-foot wonder, The Big Show, a.k.a. Paul Wight, literally broke into the WWF at their 1999 St. Valentine's Day Massacre, as he tore through the squared circle and attacked Steve Austin. The Big Show then proceeded to put on a show that no one would forget by throwing "Stone Cold" through a steel cage. The wrestler who is as big as a house wanted everyone to know he was in the house on that February night!

The two-time WWF champion doesn't need anyone to help him generate heat in between the ropes, but when he does team with another grappler, namely The Undertaker, he is even more lethal. When he teamed with The 'Taker in August 1999, the two mammoth grapplers would win the first of their two tag-team championships.

He made his professional debut in July 1995 in the WCW, where he came onto the scene billed as The Giant, supposedly Andre The Giant's long-lost son. The monster-sized wrestler made a name for himself during his time at the Atlanta-based federation; he won the WCW World Heavyweight title twice and the tag straps three times.

The Giant won his first championship match rather impressively when he defeated wrestling icon Hulk Hogan on October 29, 1995, after having been in the federation for only three months. He also made his mark on the tag ranks, garnering three belts with three different partners.

Two things are certain when it comes to Paul Wight's wrestling: he has the talent to go as far as he wants in the business and he knows how to put on a "Big Show" when he's in the ring!

BUFF BAGWELL

HEIGHT: **6'1"**
WEIGHT: **247 lbs.**
HOMETOWN: **Marietta, Georgia**
FINISHING MOVE: **Buff Blockbuster**

This guy not only has the stuff, but he is tough beyond words. Buff Bagwell proved to the wrestling world that he means to make a name for himself in this rough-and-tumble business when he came back from a ring-related injury that threatened his ability to ever walk again.

Bagwell not only has the determination to succeed between the ropes, he also has the looks, the moves and the ability to annihilate anyone in his way. He made his pro debut in the 1990 season and went on to win WCW Rookie of the Year honors.

The tremendously popular grappler has been a tag champ on

three separate occasions with three different partners and has since left the tag division looking to show his stuff off on the singles circuit. Don't put it past him to try anything between the ropes if it means it'll give him an advantage. He once entered the ring in a wheelchair three months after his near-paralyzing match with Rick Steiner just to try and trick his ring foe into believing that he couldn't walk.

Tricks or no tricks, Buff truly has the stuff not only to be popular with the fans, but more importantly to be federation champ.

AL SNOW
HEIGHT: **6'0"**
WEIGHT: **234 lbs.**
HOMETOWN: **Lima, Ohio**
FINISHING MOVE: **Snow Plow**

Who knows what's in this guy's head? Al Snow is one hell of a grappler, but he's also one crazy guy—he takes advice on his career from a mannequin head (simply known as "Head") that he carries around.

The crazy wrestler claims that the federation brass scarred him earlier in his career when they made him enter the ring under the monikers of Avatar and Leif Cassidy, and as a result, he went off the deep end. Well, whatever end he's in these days, he should stay there, as he's been having tremendous success ever since he won the Hardcore belt on April 25, 1999.

The Snowman would go on to win the hardcore strap two more times in 1999 (August 22 and September 7) and he would also win the tag title with Mankind on November 2 in Philadelphia, Pennsylvania. The Lima, Ohio, native has had memorable battles with Hardcore Holly and the Road Dogg and is currently aligned with "The Lethal Weapon" Steve Blackman.

How far this talented nutcase goes is totally up to him . . . well, not totally . . . but as long as he's thinking with the right head, he'll be fine!

DIAMOND DALLAS PAGE

HEIGHT: **6'5"**
WEIGHT: **253 lbs.**
HOMETOWN: **Point Pleasant Beach, New Jersey**
FINISHING MOVE: **Diamond-Cutter**

Diamond Dallas Page (DDP) truly knows how to generate heat. The Jersey native has worn many hats during his professional career. He went from being a nightclub owner to being a wrestling manager to being a TV color commentator to becoming a pro wrestler and eventually a grappling champion.

Page first appeared on the wrestling scene in 1988 as the manager of Badd Company (Paul Diamond and Pat Tanaka) in the AWA. He led his duo to the top of the tag mountain almost immediately, as Badd Company garnered the tag belts in March 1988. From there he moved on to do television commentary for Championship Wrestling in Florida alongside Gordon Solie.

In 1991, he hooked on with World Championship Wrestling as the manager of the tag team The Freebirds (Jimmy Garvin and Michael Hayes). Page would help this duo win the tag belts in February 1991 and he would also meet up with Diamond Studd (Scott Hall) and offer him his managing services.

In 1991, Page finally gave in to his yearnings and entered the ring as a wrestler. He first teamed with Diamond Studd and introduced himself to the fans as Diamond Dallas Page. He later teamed with Vinnie Vegas (Kevin Nash) and became associated with Scotty Flamingo (Raven). He made a name for himself as a singles wrestler by not only coming into the ring with an entourage of beautiful women known as the "Diamond Dolls," but also by kicking butt in the ring.

DDP would eventually lose his entourage of sexy chicks (well, not all of them; he would marry one of the Dolls—Kimberly Falkenberg), but that didn't stop him in his run for federation gold. During his awesome career, his lethal finishing move, the Diamond-Cutter, has helped him record seven championship titles. The six-foot-five, 253-pound wrestler has won the WCW World Heavyweight Championship, the U.S. Title and the tag-team strap all twice, and has also garnered the TV Title once.

Page is truly a diamond in the rough-and-tough wrestling world, who can make his opponents "feel the bang" whenever he steps onto the mat.

"MR. ASS" BILLY GUNN

HEIGHT: **6'4"**
WEIGHT: **268 lbs.**
HOMETOWN: **Austin, Texas**
FINISHING MOVE: **Fame-Ass-Er**

"Mr. Ass" Billy Gunn is arguably the best pound-for-pound athlete in the WWF, but that's not what's made him famous. And in case you're thinking along "badass" lines, it's not his rump, either. Gunn has found success both on the singles and tag circuits, and he has ten championship titles to his name.

Early in his career, as one-half of the Smoking Gunns duo, Billy won three tag-team championships with his brother Bart, but it wasn't until he met the "Road Dogg" Jesse Jammes, that his tag career would take off. The two joined forces and became known as the New Age Outlaws. Not only have they won five tag championships together; they are also considered one of the best twosomes ever to hit the circuit.

In his time away from the Dogg, Mr. Ass has also collected some singles titles. In 1999, the badass not only won the King of the Ring tournament, he also won the Hardcore title on March 15 in San Jose, California.

Wrestlers all over are finding out the hard way that it's not safe to play with a Gunn, especially one that won't think twice about shooting you in the "ass"!

SID VICIOUS

HEIGHT: **6'8"**
WEIGHT: **318 lbs.**
HOMETOWN: **West Memphis, Arkansas**
FINISHING MOVE: **The Powerbomb**

Sid Vicious is a wrestler who has clearly lived up to his name during his pro-wrestling career. The muscle-packed giant is not only one of the WCW's most lethal grapplers, he is also one of their most exciting.

At six-foot-eight and 318 pounds, Vicious's physical presence alone makes his opponents quiver in their boots before their match against him even begins. Whether he's facing a veteran like Hulk Hogan or a young talent like Goldberg, it doesn't matter. This blond-haired brute knows how to win.

The man, who has also gone by the ring names of Psycho Sid and Sid Justice, has several championship titles to his name, including two Heavyweight belts from both the WWF and WCW. The Arkansas native got his training from a mat technician named Tojo Yamamoto, and broke onto the wrestling scene in Memphis under the Lord Humongous moniker.

Today, this self-proclaimed "master ruler of the world" is not only one of wrestling's finest heels, he is also a key component in the future plans of the WCW. This can be both a good and bad thing for the federation.

The good thing is that Vicious is one of the grappling game's most talented stars, who can carry a federation on his broad shoulders. But the bad thing is that he has a track record of disappearing from the ring wars for some time for personal reasons and this won't help if the WCW wants to compete in the ratings and popularity wars with the WWF. So as long as Vicious is in the ring competing, there's no doubt he'll be generating heat, but if he goes "Psycho," all hell could break loose.

STEPHANIE McMAHON

HEIGHT: 5'9"

HOMETOWN: Greenwich, Connecticut

FAMOUS SAYING: "Shut up!"

Stephanie McMahon is taking the World Wrestling Federation to places it's never been before. The beautiful and intelligent controller of the WWF has aligned herself with her "husband," Triple H, and together they are not only calling the shots for the federation, but they are also the reigning men and women's champs. Triple H defended his heavyweight title at WrestleMania 2000, while Stephanie won her first women's title five days before the big WWF event in San Antonio against two-time ladies' champ Jacqueline.

Many of the other WWF members disapprove of her making the decisions, but she doesn't care. She's the boss's daughter and can do whatever the hell she wants! The youngest McMahon sibling has been getting the fans' attention for almost two years now, ever since she first came on the scene when The Undertaker starting "stalking" her. The situation only heated up when the dark warrior kidnapped her and tied her to a human-sized cross, threatening to crucify Vince's little daughter. To everyone's surprise, she was rescued by none other than WWF fan favorite, "Stone Cold" Steve Austin.

The head honcho's daughter was also engaged at one time to the wrestler known as Test, but Triple H put an end to that relationship when he supposedly "married" Stephanie in Las Vegas at one of those drive-through chapels, while she was passed out in the passenger's seat of his car.

But Stephanie doesn't seem to mind the union between her and Triple H, and if anyone dares to question their couplehood or her intentions, the WWF vixen will just tell them to "Shut up!"

ROAD DOGG

HEIGHT: **6'2"**
WEIGHT: **236 lbs.**
HOMETOWN: **Nashville, Tennessee**

Here's a guy who's as entertaining on the mic as he is in the ring. The Dogg can get the crowd going before he even tangles with his opponent, as he leads the arena crowds in their cheers!

He, like "Mr. Ass" Billy Gunn, has also found success both on the tag and singles circuits. The Nashville native not only has his five New Age Outlaw tag titles from his accomplishments with Gunn in the squared circle, but he also has won the Hardcore and Intercontinental belts.

The six-foot-two, 236-pound wrestler not only talks the talk in the WWF. He also walks the walk. Those grapplers who think that his bark is worse than his bite usually find out the hard way that this isn't true when this untamed Dogg lets loose on them.

X-PAC

HEIGHT: **6'0"**
WEIGHT: **212 lbs.**
HOMETOWN: **Minneapolis, Minnesota**
FINISHING MOVE: **X-Factor**

X-Pac marks the spot and whatever else he wants when he's in the ring. This twenty-eight-year old grappler is not only lightning-quick in between the ropes, he is also heavily armed with a great number of lethal weapons in his wrestling arsenal.

The Minnesota native may be just over two hundred pounds when he's soaking wet, but don't let that fool you. This guy can generate heat with the best of 'em. This loud, obnoxious wrestler is not afraid of any federation star and no matter their size or weight, will tell them off or throw down with them at any given opportunity.

Pac-Man, who used to be known as the clean-cut 1-2-3 Kid, has two European championships and four tag-team straps under his belt already. The shade-wearing rebel has also been part of many hell-raising factions in his career. He is currently a charter member of the WWF's infamous gang D-Generation X, and was also part of the WCW terror group known as the New World Order. Way before DX and the nWo, in his first WWF tour of duty, X-Pac was an accepted member of a clique known as the Kliq.

But whether he is alone or in a group, it doesn't matter, because the X-man usually factors in a way to make his presence known!

THE GODFATHER

HEIGHT: **6'6"**
WEIGHT: **320 lbs.**
HOMETOWN: **The Red Light District**
FINISHING MOVE: **Pimp Drop**

The Godfather has certainly proven to his opponents that "pimpin' ain't easy" and neither is tangling with the hulking 320-pound wrestler in the ring. The jewelry and colorful clothes–wearing grappler will do whatever it takes to get the win whenever he steps into an arena, as he is known as a no-holds-barred type of wrestler around the circuit.

The six-foot-six, cigar-smoking competitor not only has a love for hurting his foes; he also has an eye for spotting ho's. The WWF superstar is always being escorted to the ring by his harem of beautiful ladies known as the "Ho Train."

Before he nails his opponents with his potent Pimp Drop, he offers them some lovin' from his girls in return for the victory and if they refuse his offer, The Godfather doesn't get mad, he gets down! The powerful pimp then proceeds to give them some of his tough lovin'!

The G-man may say that "pimpin' ain't easy," but it sure looks like he's having a lot of fun doing it!

CHRIS BENOIT

HEIGHT: **5'10"**
WEIGHT: **220 lbs.**
HOMETOWN: **Edmonton, Alberta**
FINISHING MOVE: **Crippler Crossface**

Chris Benoit is an extreme wrestler who will do whatever is necessary to his opponent in the ring in order to score a victory. So it's no wonder he first made a name for himself on the Philadelphia circuit with the Extreme Championship Wrestling organization.

Growing up in Canada, he knew very early on that he wanted to become a professional wrestler, so he contacted the legendary Canadian grappler and trainer Stu Hart and asked him to teach him the ropes. When Hart agreed, Benoit made his way to Calgary and started learning his trade at Hart's school, The Dungeon.

Before making his way to ECW, the Edmonton native traveled the world and wrestled in countries like Germany, Mexico and Japan, perfecting his maneuvers. When he returned and joined on with the Philadelphia-based promotion, he immediately made a name for himself by the way he punished his opponents in the ring. Benoit would get labeled "The Crippler" for his unmerciful style on the mat and was on his way to becoming a well-respected grappler in the federation.

During his ECW days, he would not only become known as one of the most-skilled technical wrestlers in the sport; he would also gain recognition from his association with Dean Malenko. Together they would win championship gold on the tag circuit, as they knocked over any team in their way.

From Pennsylvania The Crippler moved on to Atlanta and the WCW and has had a very successful career. But after a while he tired of their competition and wanted new challenges. He bolted the federation the night after being crowned Heavyweight Champion over Sid Vicious and made his way to Stamford, Connecticut, where he currently has his sights on crippling his WWF opponents.

Tag Teams

TOO COOL

Scotty Too Hotty
HEIGHT: **5'9"**
WEIGHT: **209 lbs.**
HOMETOWN: **Westbrook, Maine**

Grandmaster Sexay
HEIGHT: **5'10"**
WEIGHT: **213 lbs.**
HOMETOWN: **Memphis, Tennessee**

Too Cool is in "da House" and is "da bomb!" This tag team has brought hip-hop to da ring, but don't let that fool you, these guys can really handle themselves between da ropes.

Grandmaster Sexay and Scotty Too Hotty may be undersized by pro wrestling standards, but what they lack in physical size they surely make up for in ego. When this dancing duo enters the arena to the blaring hip-hop music, the fans go wild, especially the women. Sometimes after their matches, they even call upon their pleasantly plump friend, Rikishi, to help them celebrate their victory, as the trio gyrates to the beat in the center of the ring.

But as much as this cocky tandem is loved by their fans, they are hated twice as much by their opponents. Grandmaster and Scotty, formerly known around the circuit as Brian Christopher and Scott Taylor, have managed to get under the skin of several other tag teams in the WWF, but they don't seem to mind. They have enough confidence in their ability to be able to get down in the ring or trash-talk their foes.

Sexay and Hotty have all the talent in the world and should strut their way to the top of the tag ranks in no time flat, but until then they'll just keep dancing their way to victory and into the hearts of their fans.

HEADBANGERS

Mosh
HEIGHT: **6'1"**
WEIGHT: **231 lbs.**
HOMESTATE: **New Jersey**

Thrasher
HEIGHT: **6'2"**
WEIGHT: **240 lbs.**
HOMESTATE: **New Jersey**

This tandem is one of the most entertaining tag teams around. They not only have the talent to go far in the tag ranks, but also know how to put on a good show with their wacky ways.

Mosh and Thrasher won the WWF Tag-Team Championship way back in 1997 in Louisville, Kentucky, when they took part in a four-way match with The Godwinns, The Legion of Doom and Owen Hart with the British Bulldog. Not long after that the two split up their team for a while, but would rejoin forces one night on an episode of *HEAT*.

The Headbangers surely live up to their name when they are between the ropes with their daring moves and no-nonsense style, but whether or not they can regain hold of the championship straps is anyone's guess. They must keep their heads in the game instead of concentrating on their wacky outfits and crazy antics if they want a chance at a title again.

MAMALUKES

Big Vito
HEIGHT: **(Don't friggin' know)**
WEIGHT: **200 sometin' lbs.**
HOMETOWN: **Brooklyn, New York**

Johnny the Bull
HEIGHT: **(Don't friggin' know)**
WEIGHT: **200 sometin' lbs.**
HOMETOWN: **Brooklyn, New York**

Who knew the Mamalukes would gain this much attention and this much success so fast in the WCW? After all, they only came to Atlanta to collect on a debt owed by Disco Inferno to an Italian family in Brooklyn.

Instead of cooperating with Big Vito and Johnny the Bull, Disco Inferno decided to take matters into his own hands, so he called upon his archrival Lash Leroux to help him put a hurtin' on the two thugs from Brooklyn. Not a wise move.

Inferno and Leroux should have shown the two hitmen a little more respect than that, as they would pay for their knucklehead maneuvers a short while later. Not only would the Mamalukes rough up this pair, they would go on and win the WCW tag belts from David Flair and Crowbar on January 18, 1999, in Evansville, Indiana, after only being on the federation circuit for a couple of weeks.

In typical Mamaluke fashion, the duo is ecstatic to be the reigning WCW tag champs, but they are also bummed, because now they won't be able to watch their favorite TV show, *The Sopranos,* because they will be in the ring defending their title.

THE DUDLEY BOYZ

D-Von
HEIGHT: **6'2"**
WEIGHT: **240 lbs.**
HOMETOWN: **Dudleyville**

Buh Buh Ray
HEIGHT: **6'4"**
WEIGHT: **275 lbs.**
HOMETOWN: **Dudleyville**

This awesome twosome just arrived on the WWF scene after a four-year Extreme Championship Wrestling stint. Almost immediately, they let their competition know that "thou shall not mess with the Dudleys!" While this pair may be successful in the ring, they don't have many friends or fans outside the squared circle.

Throughout their career they have had a reputation for being crude, crass and vulgar toward their opponents and blatantly disrespectful to the audience. The five-time ECW tag champions claim to be the best tag tandem in the business and they dare anyone to prove them wrong.

So far, they've backed up their words in the WWF—they won the tag championship straps from the five-time tag-belt-holding New Age Outlaws in Hartford, Connecticut, on February 27, 2000.

This lethal pair should battle for the tag straps for a long time to come, as they not only possess one of wrestling's most-feared finishing moves in the 3-D—the Dudley Death Drop—they also have six championship titles to back up their words. "Thou shall not mess with the Dudleys!"

THE HARDY BOYZ

Matt Hardy
HEIGHT: **6'1"**
WEIGHT: **220 lbs.**
HOMETOWN: **Cameron, North Carolina**

Jeff Hardy
HEIGHT: **6'1"**
WEIGHT: **212 lbs.**
HOMETOWN: **Cameron, North Carolina**

The Hardy Boyz had their coming out party on October 17, 1999, at a No Mercy Pay-Per-View at the Gund Arena in Cleveland, Ohio, where they squared off in a ladder match against another up-and-coming tag-team duo, Edge and Christian.

The match between the pairs was to be a memorable one, since the four young warriors would battle not only for a $100,000 cash prize, but the winner would also walk away with the managerial services of the vivacious Terri Runnels.

The team would not only walk away that night with Terri, the loot and the victory; they would also win over thousands of fans with their high-flying acrobatic moves. The youthful grapplers proved on this night that not only could they wrestle with Edge (and Christian), but they could also perform on the edge and keep the fans at the edge of their seats!

Matt and Jeff are not only two of the youngest wrestlers on the scene today, they are also one of the most talented tandems in the federation today. Having Terri in their corner should only help pave their way to the top of championship mountain. But even without the gorgeous bombshell, this duo is destined for stardom.

THE HOLLY COUSINS

Hardcore Holly
HEIGHT: **6'6" (?)**
WEIGHT: **400 (?) lbs.**
HOMETOWN: **Mobile, Alabama**

Crash Holly
HEIGHT: **6'6" (?)**
WEIGHT: **400 (?) lbs.**
HOMETOWN: **Mobile, Alabama**

This tag team has proven that not only is wrestling in their blood, but also insanity! Both Hardcore Holly and Crash Holly have the same delusion that they should not be wrestling any competition under six-foot-six, four-hundred-pounds. They have even been known to carry a scale to the ring to weigh their opponents before the bout to see if they meet their criteria.

The Holly Cousins have proven to the wrestling world that they are capable of holding championship titles—Hardcore is the holder of five career titles and Crash is the owner of two; but now they need to show that they are of sound mind to wrestle. Once they stop wrestling against the impossible and start going after wrestlers from their own weight class, this "hardcore" family duo should rack up titles and wins for a long time to come.

THE ACOLYTES

Bradshaw
HEIGHT: **6'6"**
WEIGHT: **290 lbs.**

Faarooq
HEIGHT: **6'2"**
WEIGHT: **270 lbs.**

This is one tag team you don't want to have mad at you. The Acolytes are not only two-time WWF Tag-Team Champions; they are also two of the most feared wrestlers on the circuit today.

One-half of the tough tandem is occupied by Bradshaw, who first came to prominence as a member of The Blackjacks with Barry Windham. He then helped Taka Michinoku in his feud with the Kaiental clan. The monstrous wrestler then teamed up with Faarooq as one of The Acolytes and together they took on the tag ranks.

The second half of the bone-bending squad is Faarooq, a former professional football player who founded the Nation of Domination. The master of chaos was also once a world Heavyweight Champion in the WCW, when he wrestled under his real name, Ron Simmons.

The last time this pair won the tag title was on July 25, 1999, in Buffalo, New York, but you can bet your last dollar on the fact that this mean team will once again wear federation gold!

EDGE AND CHRISTIAN

Edge
HEIGHT: **6'4"**
WEIGHT: **240 lbs.**
HOMETOWN: **Toronto, Canada**

Christian
HEIGHT: **5'10"**
WEIGHT: **215 lbs.**
HOMETOWN: **Toronto, Canada**

This is a team that you will be hearing a lot about not only in the tag circuit, but in the singles ranks as well. Edge and Christian both have talent and youth on their side, and judging from the reaction they get when they come into the ring, expect for them to get a serious push for the tag title some time soon.

The dynamic duo combines good looks, high-flying maneuvers and a fearless attitude in the ring that has made them popular not only with the fans (especially the young ladies), but also with their peers.

Edge and Christian proved that they could generate some awesome heat between the ropes when they squared off against The Hardy Boyz in an unforgettable ladder match on October 17, 1999. Even though they lost the No Mercy Pay-Per-View event to the Boyz, they earned both their foes' and the fans' respect that night.

The former Brood members performed maneuvers well above the mat on this night, which would be a sign of things to come. They think nothing of putting their bodies on the line for the sake of the recording the win.

Even though these two young Canadian grapplers have yet to wear the Tag-Team Champion straps, you can expect to see them on top of the duo circuit before the year is out.

NEW AGE OUTLAWS

"Road Dogg" Jesse Jammes
HEIGHT: **6'2"**
WEIGHT: **236 lbs.**
HOMETOWN: **Nashville, Tennessee**

"Mr. Ass" Billy Gunn
HEIGHT: **6'4"**
WEIGHT: **268 lbs.**
HOMETOWN: **Austin, Texas**

The New Age Outlaws are a tag team that is a true force to be reckoned with on the tag-team circuit—they are the proud winners of five WWF Tag Championship titles. Both of these wrestlers have the talent to be winners on not only the tag circuit but also in the singles ranks.

Learn to expect the unexpected from this rebellious duo, as they've been known to cause havoc outside the ring as well as inside the ropes. For more info on these DX outlaws, check out the Heat Generators section in this book.

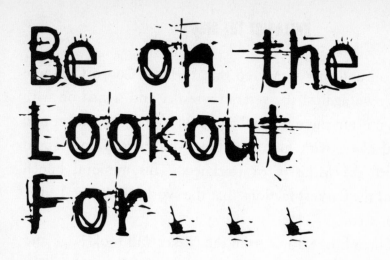

Be on the Lookout For...

EDGE

HEIGHT: 6'4"
WEIGHT: 240 lbs.
HOMETOWN: Toronto, Canada
FINISHING MOVE: Downward Spiral

Edge is the type of wrestler who lives up to his name, because he keeps both his fans and opponents on the edge! The long-haired grappler first came to the WWF when he was discovered by Carl DeMarco in Whitby, Ontario, where he was wrestling on a card for an independent federation.

DeMarco really liked what he saw from the young grappler, as he was using his quickness and all kinds of aerial acrobatics on his opponent Joey Legend that evening. A short time later, Edge would get a call from DeMarco telling him to come down to a WWF event because they wanted to try him out in a match against Bob Holly.

Edge went and met DeMarco that night at Copps Coliseum and held his own against the veteran wrestler and signed on with the federation. From there he hooked up with The Undertaker and was inducted along with his other blood brothers, Gangrel and Christian, into the Ministry of Darkness. This immoral bunch formed one of the darkest factions that the World Wrestling Federation has ever seen.

Gangrel then broke away from the 'Taker and took Edge and Christian with him and formed a gothic group known as The Brood. This terrifying trio would raise hell on some of the organization's most popular stars and would be involved in some of the bloodiest matches ever to take place in the WWF.

The Toronto native then branched out on his own and won the Intercontinental title in storybook fashion in front of his hometown fans at the sold-out SkyDome on July 24, 1999, against Jeff Jarrett.

The gothic warrior, along with Christian, is also one-half of one of wrestling's most talented and electrifying duos. These young matsmen should not only dominate the tags for years to come, they also should have a very big impact on the future of the singles ranks.

BILLY KIDMAN

HEIGHT: **5'11"**
WEIGHT: **195 lbs.**
HOMETOWN: **Allentown, Pennsylvania**
FINISHING MOVE: **Shooting Star Press**

Billy Kidman is truly one of World Championship Wrestling's up-and-comers who will carry wrestling into the new millennium. The twenty-six-year old grappler has paid his dues over the years, wrestling on the independent circuit and in the ECW before hooking on with the WCW.

The five-foot-eleven, 195-pound wrestler has been battling not only his in-ring foes all his career, but the skeptics as well. Time and time again he has had to prove himself in the world of giants that he works in that he's not too small to tangle with the big boys.

The Pennsylvania native has already won the Cruiserweight championship twice and has also held the tag belt once with his ring-partner Konnan. But those belts should be just the beginning for the only WCWer who can perform the dreaded finishing move called the Shooting Star Press.

The only thing that could stop Kidman from climbing the ladder of success in wrestling is himself . . . or his love for the beautiful ladies.

RIKISHI PHATU

HEIGHT: 6'1"
WEIGHT: 423 lbs.
HOMETOWN: Samoa
FINISHING MOVE: Sit-down Piledriver

Making his second go-ROUND in the WWF, Rikishi has not only captured the hearts of the fans; he has also pulverized anyone who has had the nerve to step foot in the ring with him.

The big blonde in a thong is a former tag-team champion from his days as a Headshrinker, but this time a-ROUND he has his eyes set on a much BIGger prize—the WWF Heavyweight Championship. The native of Samoa has a Phat finishing move called the Sit-down Piledriver, which literally crushes his opponents upon impact.

This four-hundred-pound grappling giant can also be found gyrating to the beat with the hip-hop dancing duo Too Cool. Phatu is definitely large and in charge of his own destiny and in no time he'll be one of the BIGGEST personalities in sports entertainment.

KURT ANGLE

HEIGHT: **6'2"**
WEIGHT: **220 lbs.**
HOMETOWN: **Pittsburgh, Pennsylvania**
FINISHING MOVE: **Rolling Takeover**

Kurt Angle is a wrestler who once did his country proud by winning a gold medal in the 1996 Olympic Games in Atlanta. He won the ultimate prize by dominating the 220-pound freestyle wrestling event.

Look for the Pittsburgh native not only to continue to have success between the ropes, but also on the mic. This cocky grappler has the ability to pummel his opponents, and also has the personality to get under the fans' skin and rile them up into a frenzy.

Angle is certainly the real deal, as his winning both the European and Intercontinental championships almost overnight demonstrates. Don't expect him to turn down any challenges! This Olympian has too much pride to walk away from any confrontation.

What "angles" the WWF chooses to use the full-of-himself wrestler in is anybody's guess, but you can bet your patriotic butt that he'll be wearing some more gold in the future.

EDDY GUERRERO

HEIGHT: **5'8"**
WEIGHT: **220 lbs.**
HOMETOWN: **El Paso, Texas**
FINISHING MOVE: **Frog Splash**

For Eddy Guerrero it's not a question of whether he'll make it big in wrestling, but when. This Texas native has what it takes to be a force on the pro circuit but he just can't seem to stay healthy long enough to prove it.

One of his main reasons for getting hurt a lot is that he is a risk taker. For example, when he left the WCW and joined the WWF as a member of the Radicals, he got injured in his first official match in his new federation as he was trying to deliver his famous finishing maneuver, The Frog Splash, on his opponent and landed wrong.

Once he gets well, there's no telling what he can accomplish in the ring. Guerrero comes from a wrestling family and will settle for nothing less than championship gold in his future. Before he came over to the WWF, he held several championship titles in the WCW, including the U.S. and the Cruiserweight belts.

If he can shake the injury bug during his career, there's no telling how far he can go with his talents and background. Expect Guerrero to go back to his high-flying aerial maneuvers when he comes back and watch him knock off his opponents in style.

There's no doubt that this grappler, who has wrestling in his blood, will be wearing gold around his waist for many years to come.

Did You Know...

Al Snow's real name is Allen Sarven?

**Kurt Angle considers himself to be the
only true athlete in the WWF?**

The Big Show (Paul Wight) went to
Wichita State University on a basketball
scholarship?

Billy Gunn was also known on the wrestling circuit
as "Rockabilly" at one time?

**Bradshaw of the Acolytes started his
career as a cowboy-type wrestler
known as John Hawk?**

Bret Hart was once part owner of the
Calgary Hitmen minor league hockey team
with the New York Rangers' Theoren Fleury
and the Colorado Avalanche's Joe Sakic?

Buff Bagwell once wrestled under the names the
Handsome Stranger and Marcus Alexander Bagwell?

**Chris Benoit once wore a mask in the ring and
wrestled under the name The Pegasus Kid?**

Christian and Edge have been friends ever since
the fifth grade?

Edge entered a wrestling contest in the *Toronto
Star* when he was seventeen years old and won the
chance to train for free at a wrestling school?

Chyna is the real-life girlfriend of Triple H?

Diamond Dallas Page once appeared in Stuck
Mojo's music video for the song "Rising"?

Kidman was the first wrestler to land the Shooting
Star Press on American National television?

**Eddy Guerrero's dad Gori was a superstar
wrestler in Mexico?**

Faarooq (Ron Simmons) played college football for
Florida State, and was the first Seminole defender
ever to have his jersey number retired?

The Godfather originally entered the WWF as a
voodoo character named Papa Shango?

**Goldberg's face was painted on the hood of
Jerry Nadeau's racing car, sponsored by the
WCW, which raced in the Pepsi 400
in Daytona Beach last year?**

Hardcore Holly is a former NASCAR racing driver?

Chris Jericho performs with members of the band
Stuck Mojo under the band name Fozzy Osbourne
whenever he has the time?

**Jeff Jarrett worked as a referee before he
became a pro wrestler?**

The Rock's favorite movie is *The Godfather*?

Ric Flair broke his back in a plane crash and was
told he would never wrestle again?

**Lex Luger was trained for ring action
by Hiro Matsuda?**

Kane (Glen Jacobs) used to wrestle under the
name Isaac Yankem, the evil dentist, before he
became the Big Red Machine?

Mankind's partner in crime is Mr. Socko, a home-made puppet made out of a sweat sock that he wears on his right hand?

Kevin Nash has appeared in episodes of ABC's *Sabrina, The Teenage Witch* and Nickelodeon's *Weinerville*?

Scott Hall started out his career in 1984 wrestling under the moniker of Coyote?

Hulk Hogan was even a big baby—he tipped the scales at ten pounds when he was born?

Sting made one of the most dramatic wrestling appearances on March 19, 1998, during a Thursday Thunder when he was lowered down from a helicopter into the ring?

"Stone Cold" Steve Austin announced his engagement to Debra McMichael on Super Bowl Sunday during Halftime Heat?

The Undertaker (Mark Calloway) also wrestled under the names The Master of Pain and The Punisher?

X-Pac also wrestled under the name the Lightning
Kid at one time in his career?

Sid Vicious first competed under the name Lord
Humongous on the Memphis circuit?

**Triple H and Chyna kept their boyfriend-girlfriend
relationship a secret from the
other wrestlers for ten months?**

Road Dogg's real name is Brian James?

Robert Picarello is an associate sports editor for five different professional sports publications. The St. John's graduate not only edits magazines, including *Wrestling World, Baseball Illustrated, Hockey Illustrated, Basketball Illustrated* and *Football Illustrated,* he is also a freelance sports writer who has written features for prestigious sports titles like *Yankees Magazine.*